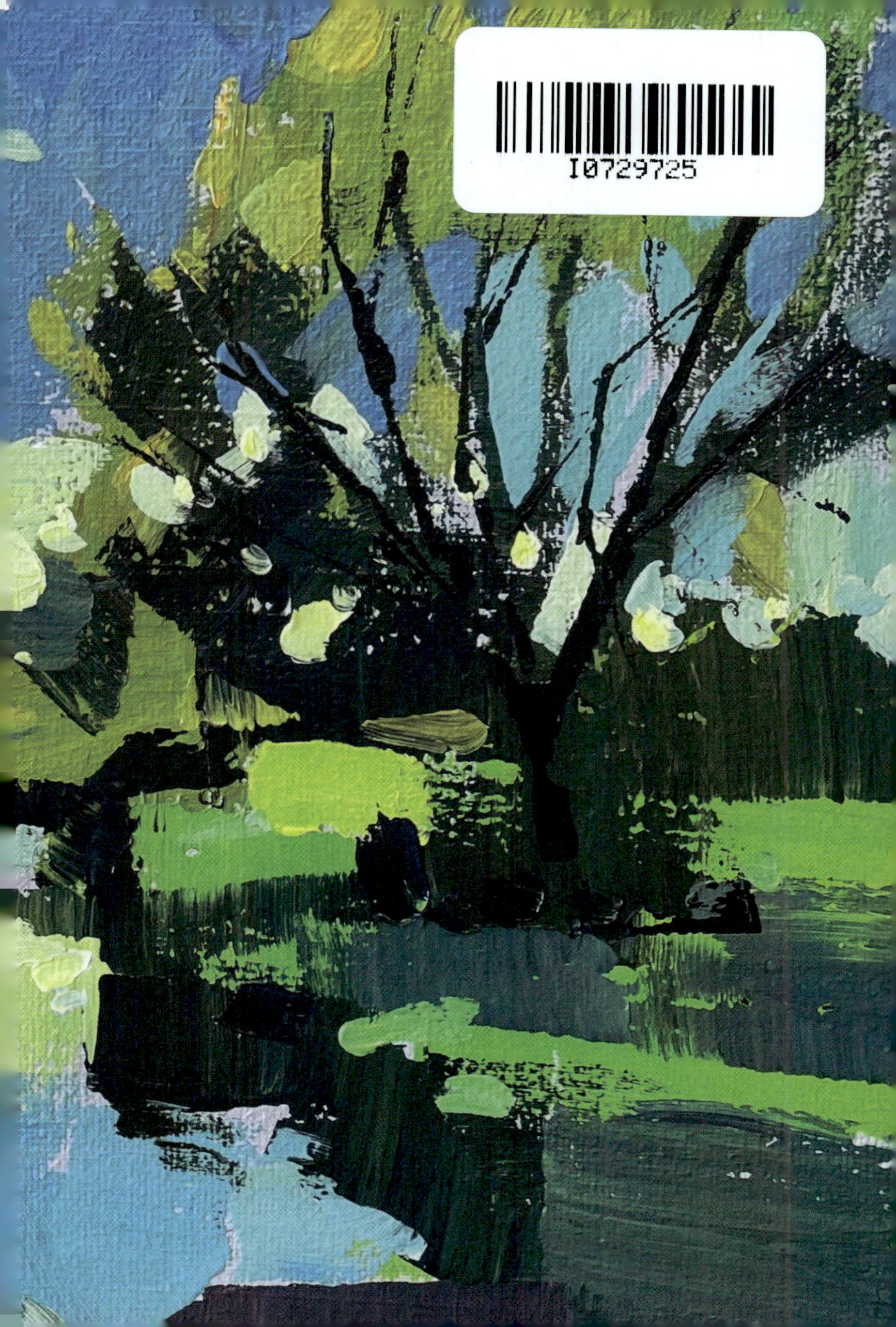
I0729725

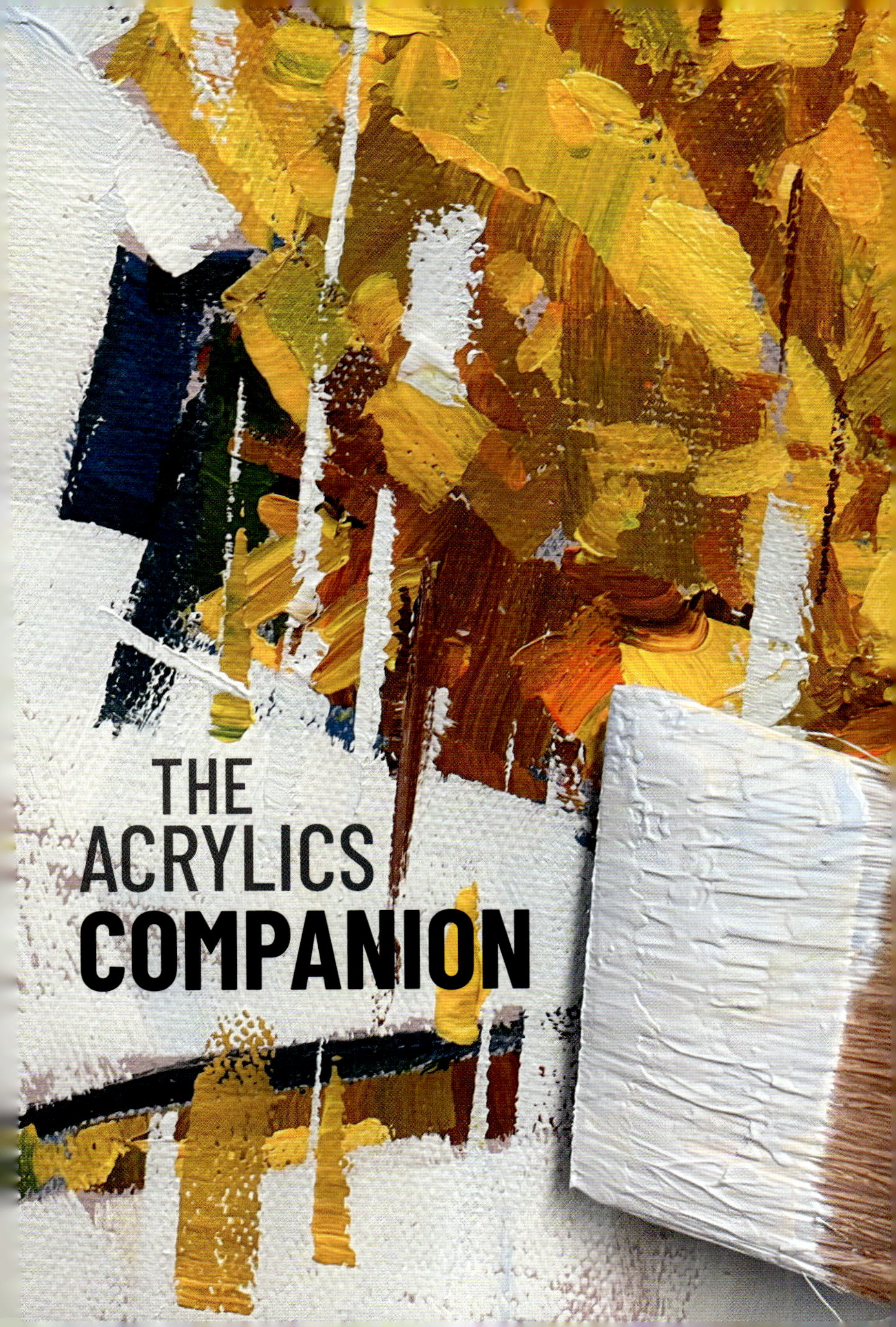
THE
ACRYLICS
COMPANION

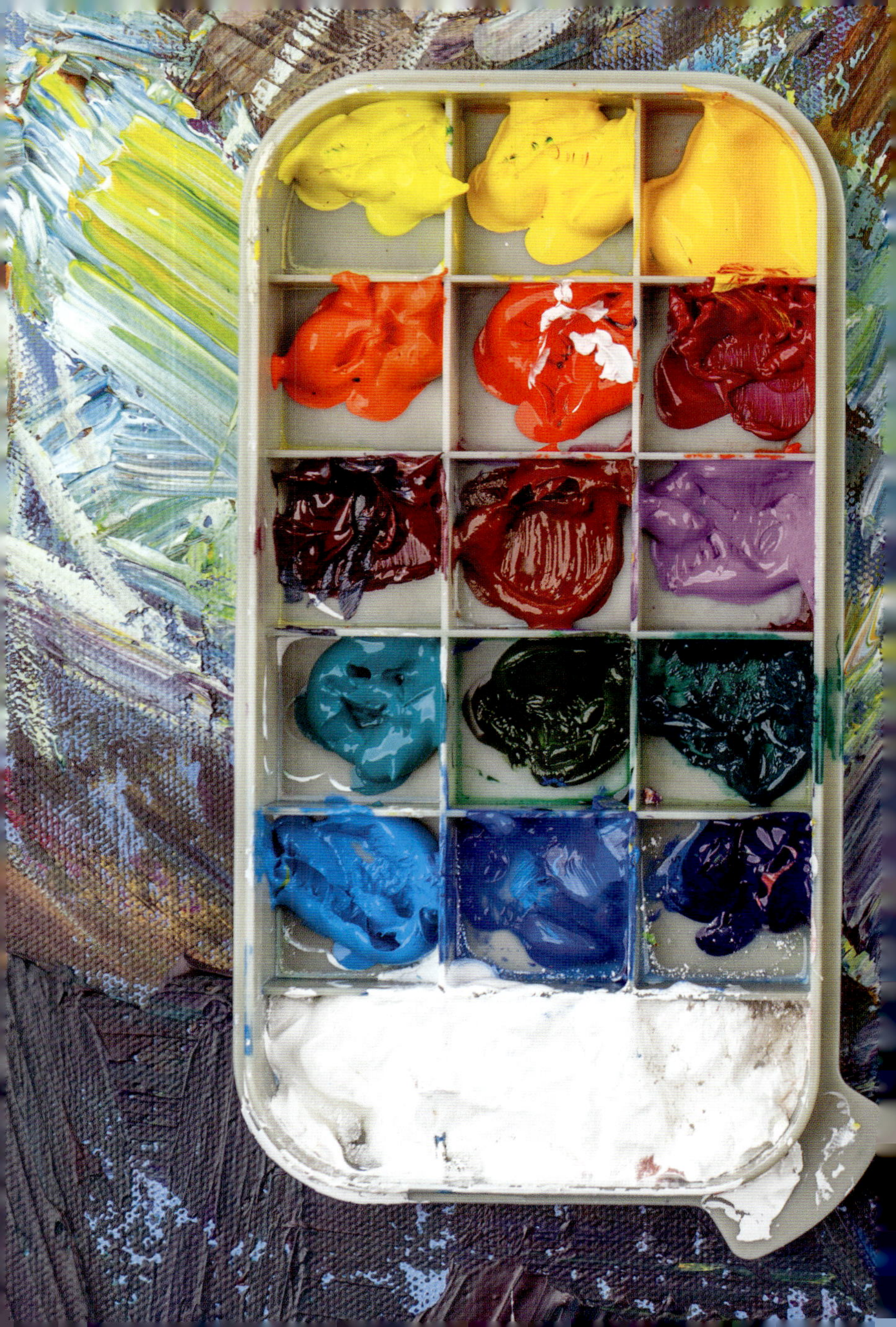

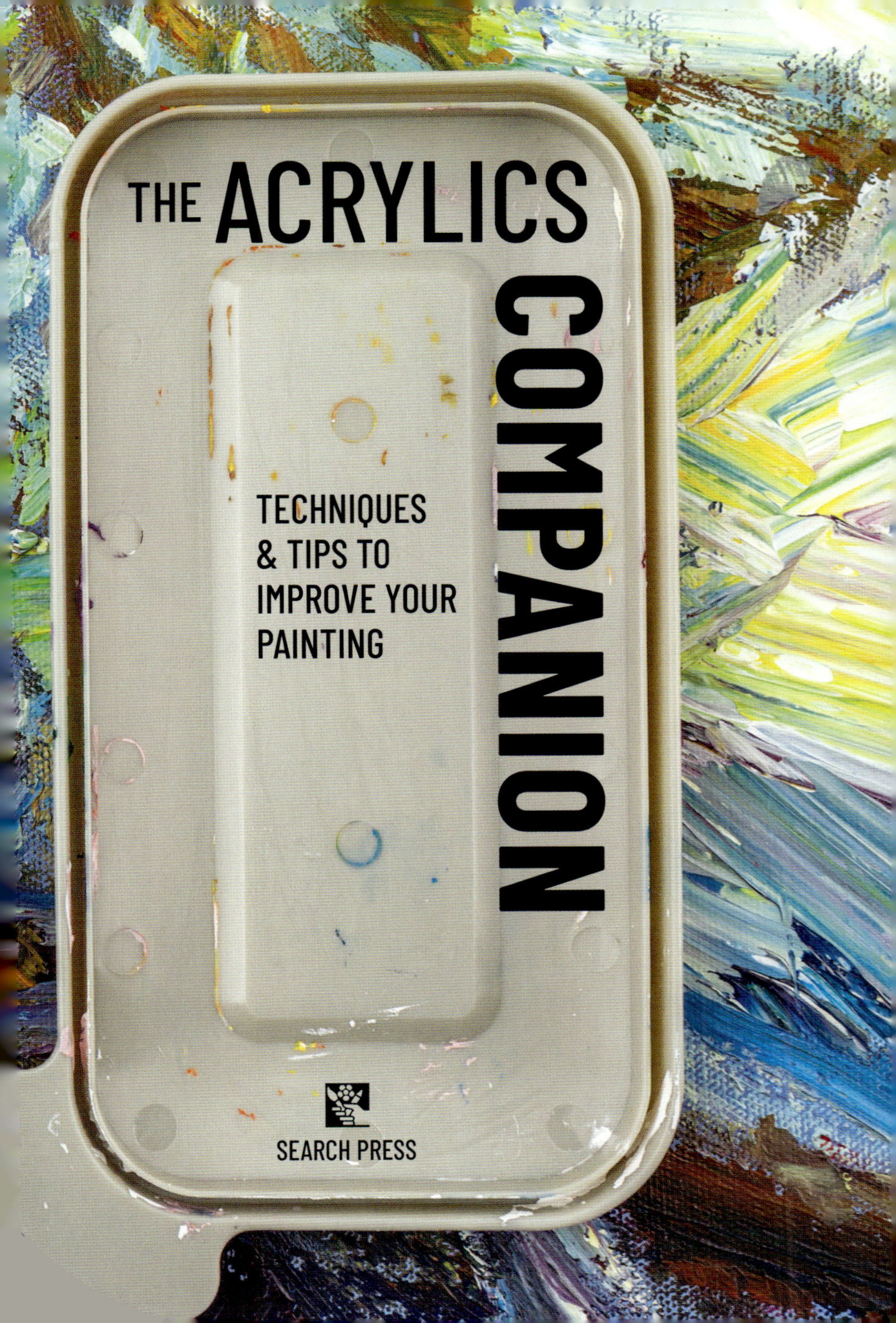

THE ACRYLICS
COMPANION
TECHNIQUES
& TIPS TO
IMPROVE YOUR
PAINTING
SEARCH PRESS

CONTENTS

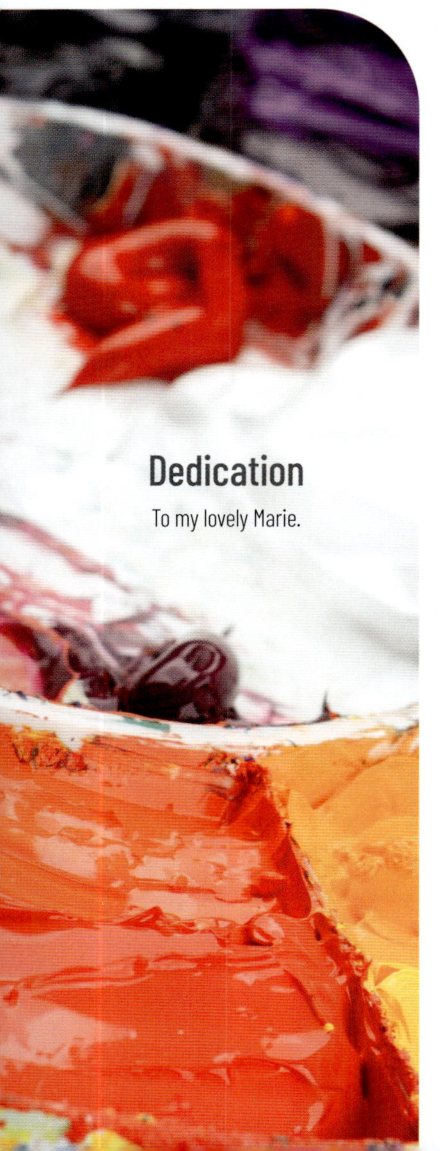

Dedication

To my lovely Marie.

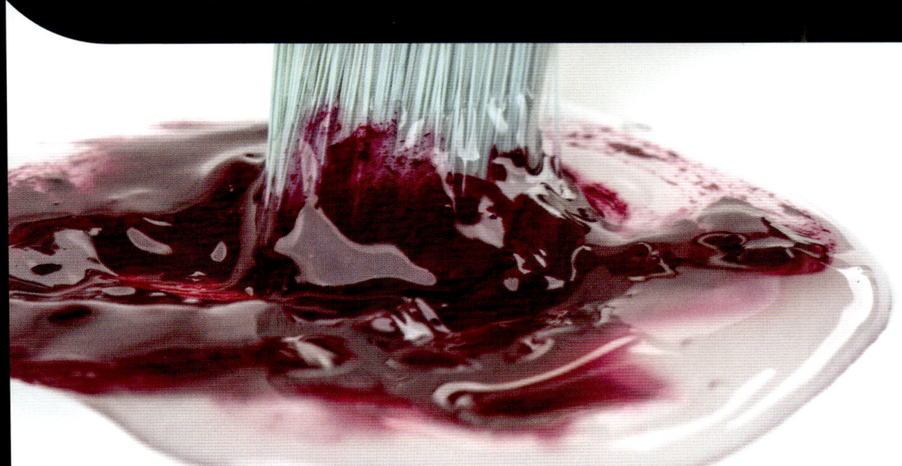

Getting started

Artists who have great affection for oil or watercolour painting sometimes criticize acrylics for the 'plastic' feel of the pigment, the vibrancy of the colours, or the fact that acrylics dry to an opaque, matt finish, quite unlike the satin lustre of oils or the transparent luminosity of watercolours. Most of these 'problems', however, are exactly why I like them. Exposed brush marks and a matt finish, for example, are reminiscent of Impressionist paintings – and that group of artists revolutionized the art world.

Forget the comparisons to oils or watercolour. Acrylics don't quite fit in either category – and have plenty of strengths of their own. You'll discover over the following pages the uniqueness of acrylics and the best way to get the most out of this versatile and exciting medium.

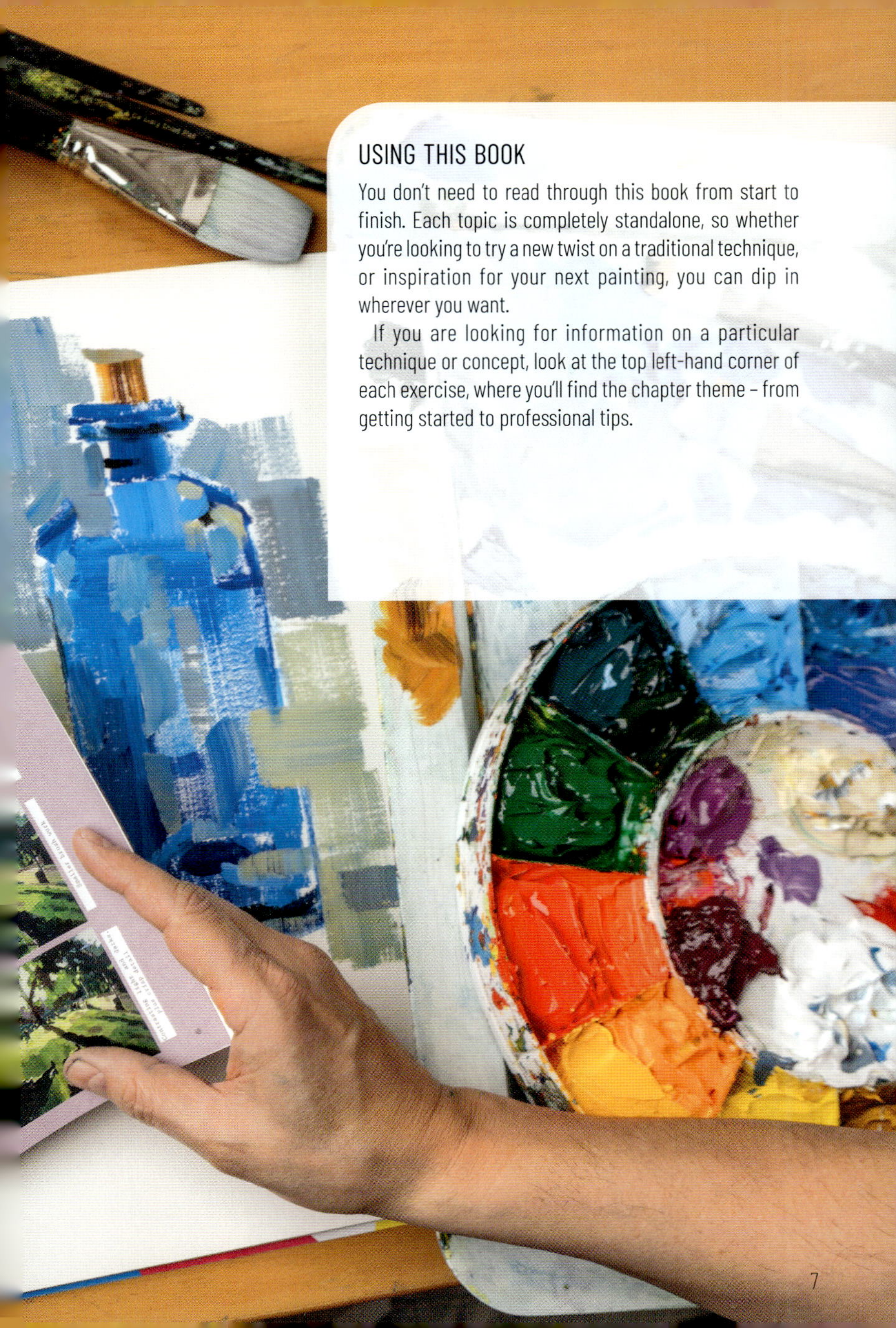

USING THIS BOOK

You don't need to read through this book from start to finish. Each topic is completely standalone, so whether you're looking to try a new twist on a traditional technique, or inspiration for your next painting, you can dip in wherever you want.

If you are looking for information on a particular technique or concept, look at the top left-hand corner of each exercise, where you'll find the chapter theme – from getting started to professional tips.

Neat paint

Used straight from the tube, acrylics are ideal for impasto effects and textures.

Acrylics – what's the fuss?

WHAT ARE ACRYLIC PAINTS?

Acrylics are pigments suspended in an air-drying plastic carrier. They are waterbased paints that dry to a durable finish which usually can't be reworked once dry. You'll find the speedy drying times of acrylic help to build up momentum from start to finish of each artwork. There's not too much maintenance when your painting is finished as you can simply clean brushes with soapy water.

WHAT TO BUY?

Acrylics can be purchased in many forms and consistencies, including ink forms or in soft, fluid consistencies. However, since any acrylics can be easily diluted to the consistency you want, but cannot so easily be thickened, I recommend buying heavy body acrylics. They offer you more options, and thus more scope in your artwork.

You can buy individual pots or tubes, or you can pick up a starter set of 6–12 acrylic colours at a reasonable cost, which will give you all you need to start.

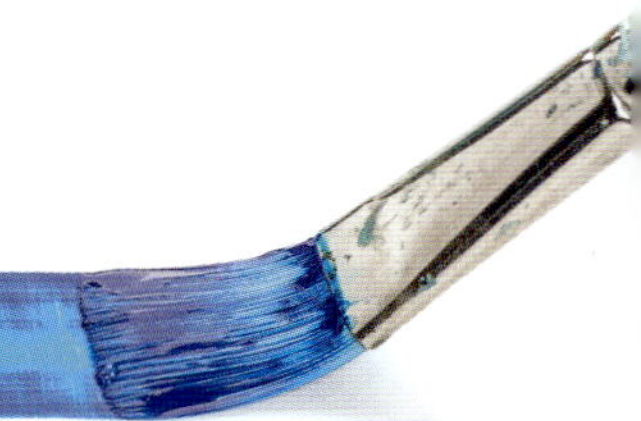

Thin paint

Acrylics can be diluted with water for thin,
transparent layers.

CHARACTERISTICS OF ACRYLIC PAINTS

Versatile Acrylics can do more than any other medium. They allow you to paint in a multitude of different ways on different surfaces.

Forgiving If you're new to painting, you will find acrylics are incredibly forgiving – you can simply paint over mistakes and be ready to paint again minutes later.

Swift and spontaneous The paint dries rapidly, allowing paintings to be completed in one sitting. So rapid, in fact, that drying times are too quick to allow for any substantial blending or reworking. Smooth, gradated layering is curtailed as the fast drying acrylic showcases more exposed brushwork.

Vibrant The vibrant colours make up for the darker variations in drying. The feel of the paint can be enhanced or elaborated on by the addition of mediums you can purchase separately.

Adaptable Acrylics require no exotic diluents; just water. There is also a huge range of specialist additive mediums (see page 33 for more on mediums). Overuse of these can be gimmicky and limiting, but used sparingly they give you still more options.

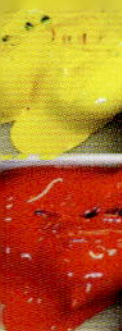

Your paint palette

The most important aspects to any acrylic palette are a lid (preferably airtight) and deep wells: when you expose acrylics to a warm environment the paint will start drying. A palette with deeper wells will help conserve the freshness of the paint for longer. It also helps if you squeeze out a little more pigment as small amounts can dry quicker.

I have a couple of palettes, a small travelling one for painting outdoors and a large circular size for regular studio painting sessions. My regular palette is called a Radial Sorting Tray, shown below. Nibble selection trays for snacks work as a surprisingly good alternative to this sort of palette (once you've eaten the nuts!). These often include lids.

Radial sorting tray

12 wells with a large central area for mixing.

Sadly, this palette doesn't come with a lid – but I've found a cake stand fits quite well.

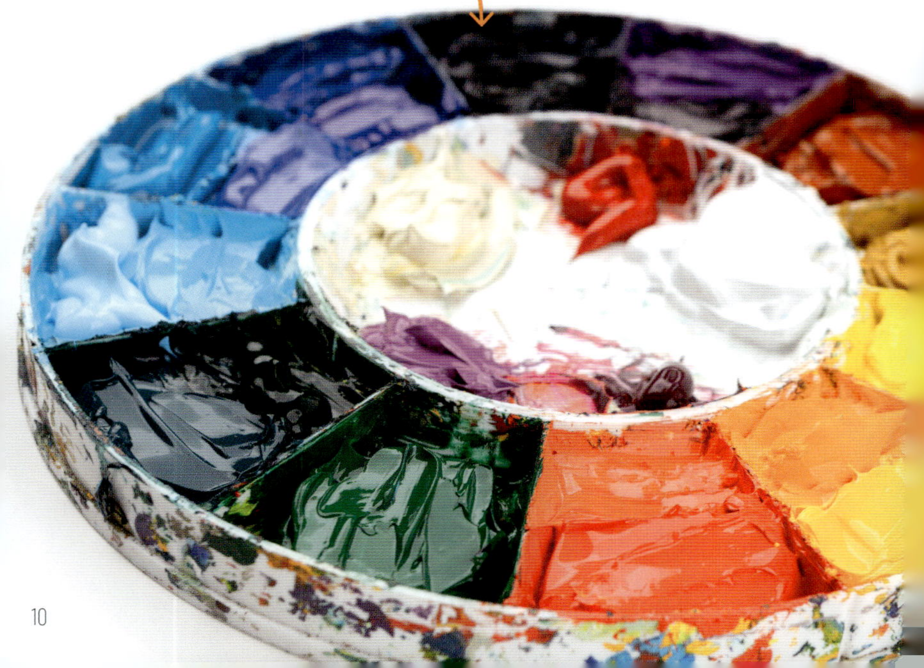

CARING FOR YOUR PAINT

- When not in use, cover the palette with a firm piece of cardboard or lid of some kind. Don't use food wrap: it can sag and dip into the paint.
- If the paint begins to firm up, just prod the pigment with a palette knife to loosen it up again.
- Keep your palette of paint away from radiators or direct sunlight.
- Keep the palette in a cool place if possible. In hot climates, spray your palette with water or liquid retarder from a diffuser – but not too much.

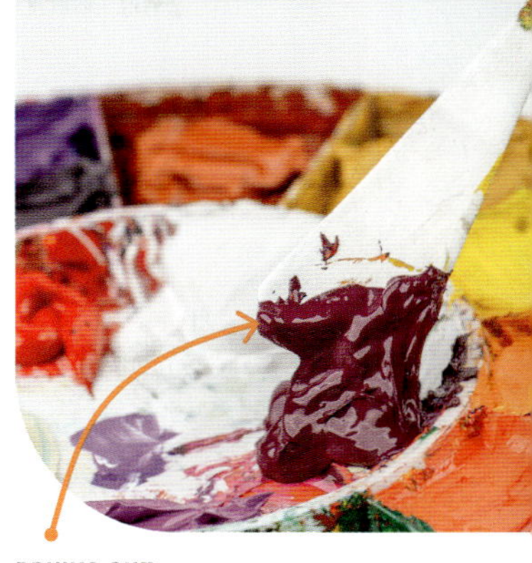

DRYING OUT

I use a lot of paint as I paint most days. To avoid waste, rather than clear and refill wells each time, I use a palette knife to skim muddied paint away from the well, then top up that colour.

When travelling, you can pop the palette in a plastic bag.

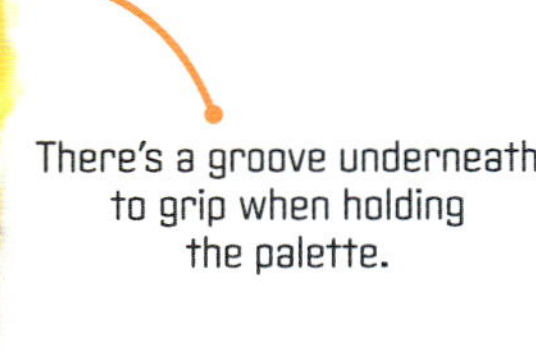

There's a groove underneath to grip when holding the palette.

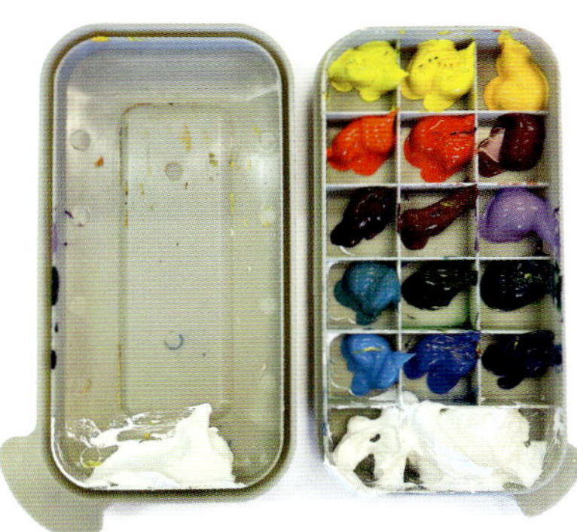

POCKET-SIZED PORTABLE PALETTE

My travel palette is fairly small, but it includes the all-important features: a tight-fitting lid and small but deep wells.

Acrylics in a nutshell

This simple tree silhouette is the perfect introduction to using acrylics. You'll need three or four acrylic colours – I'm using violet, green, blue and white – a flat brush, paper and some water. You can use almost any surface; I'm using acrylic paper.

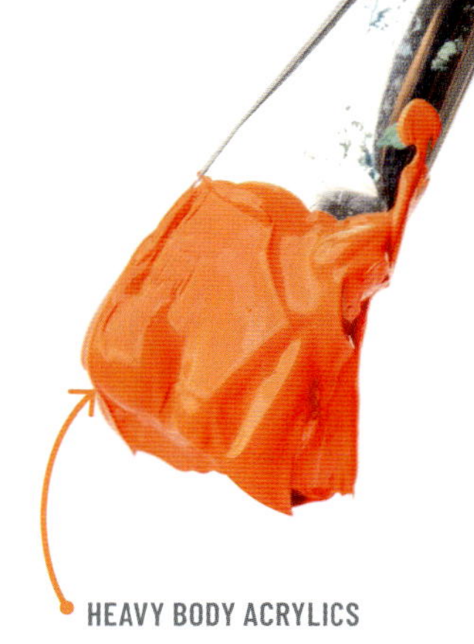

HEAVY BODY ACRYLICS

These are thick, viscous acrylic paints that are great for textural effects when used neat – but you can dilute them with water for thin, transparent layers too.

Sky

Use a mix of white and blue with just a little water to help the colours run together.

Ground

A generous amount of green, spread evenly, forms your foreground.

__STAGE 1__ Prepare your paint using just enough water to create a slightly transparent wash with exposed brushstrokes, then paint two areas as shown. Allow to dry for a few minutes.

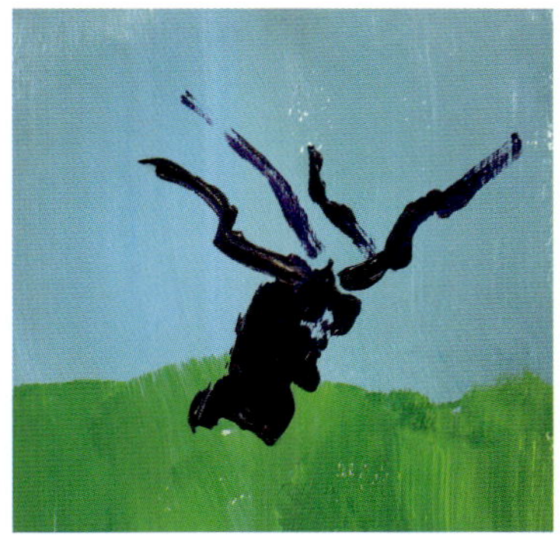

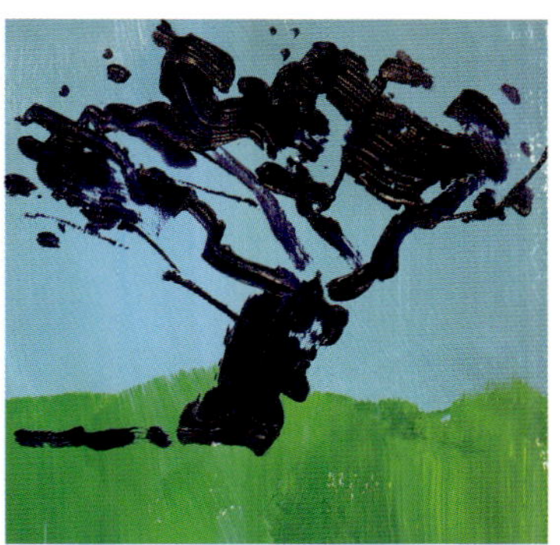

STAGE 2 Once dry, scoop up neat dark violet with a bone-dry flat brush. Starting with the main tree trunk, lightly drag a large diagonal line with the width of the brush from top to bottom. Add shorter diagonal strokes to mimic various branches, vary the sizes and apply a few twists, all with neat paint.

STAGE 3 Scoop more neat violet and gently skim where the clumps of leaves would be. It helps to angle the brush down towards the paper so more of the brush is utilized. Add little dabs for loose leaves, giving an impression of leaves blowing in the wind.

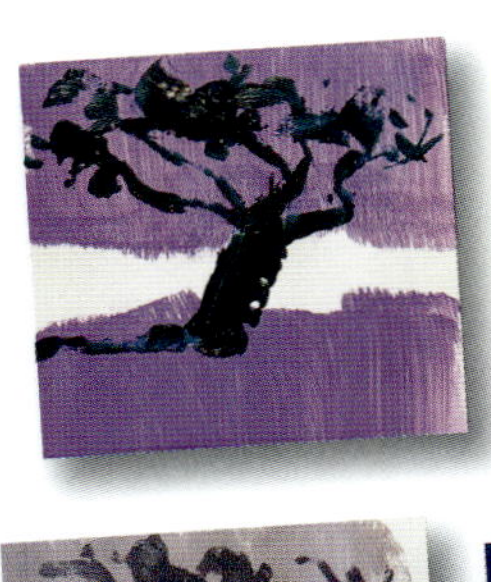

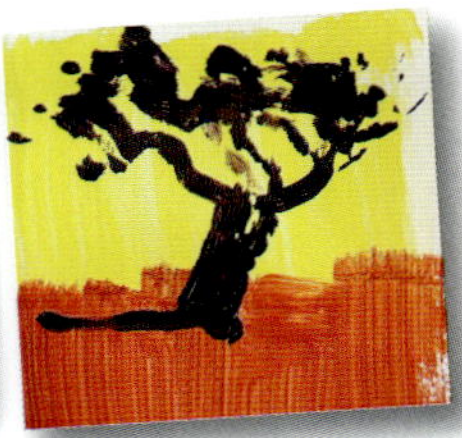

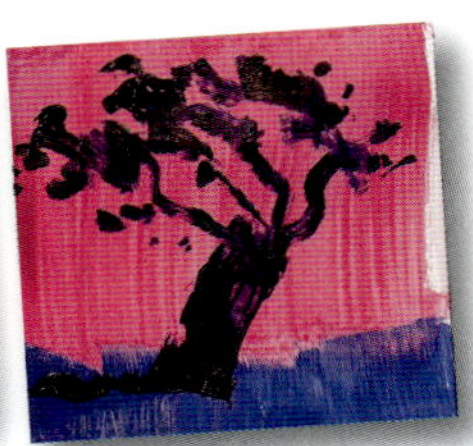

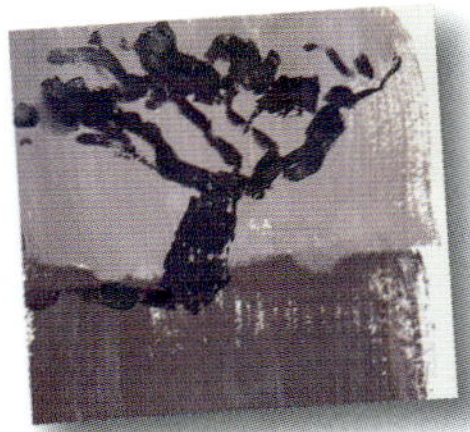

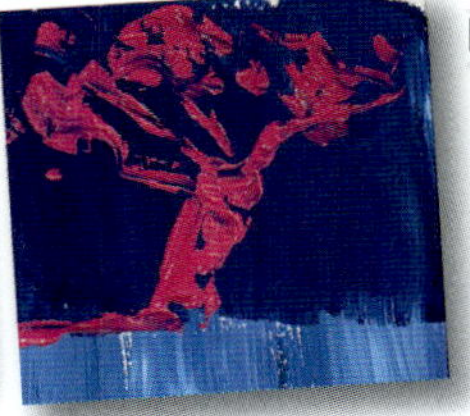

Get to know your paint

Try this same exercise using different colours for different moods.

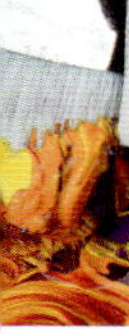

Brush up on the basics

BRUSH SHAPES

Acrylic brushes vary from traditional rounded shapes, semi-round, flats, angled or fan-like – the shape of the brush will affect the marks you are able to make with it. Here are some common types:

Riggers The extra length on the fine bristles of this brush type helps to create continuous, flexible linework, well-suited to diluted acrylics. I find this brush ideal for drawing outlines.

Rounds A good traditional all-rounder of a brush, rounds will take large loads of paint and come to a fine point for detail. The rounded shape makes blending easier.

Filberts A flat brush, but with a semi-rounded head. Filberts provide more versatility when you want a direct mark with the rounded edge to mould or blend colours together. I think of these as a luxury rather than an essential.

Flats I always recommend large flat brushes for the pronounced brushstrokes they make when applied with confidence. Particularly in the early stages of a painting, the big definite marks they create really get the engine going and create momentum behind each painting.

Angled An angled flat brush is as useful as a standard flat brush to fill in large areas, while its angled edge provides more control for finer linework. There is more precision with this brush in comparison with the traditional flat – but for looser artwork you may want to avoid that temptation.

LONG OR SHORT HAIR?

I have a varied array of short- and long-haired brushes. Longer hairs provide more bounce as you apply paint, while shorter bairs make it easier to produce controlled, concise marks.

The length of the hairs makes a big difference to the quality of the line. Small flats are good for details or edging shapes with lovely crisp lines. Flats with shorter bristles are sometimes known as 'brights' to distinguish them from long flats.

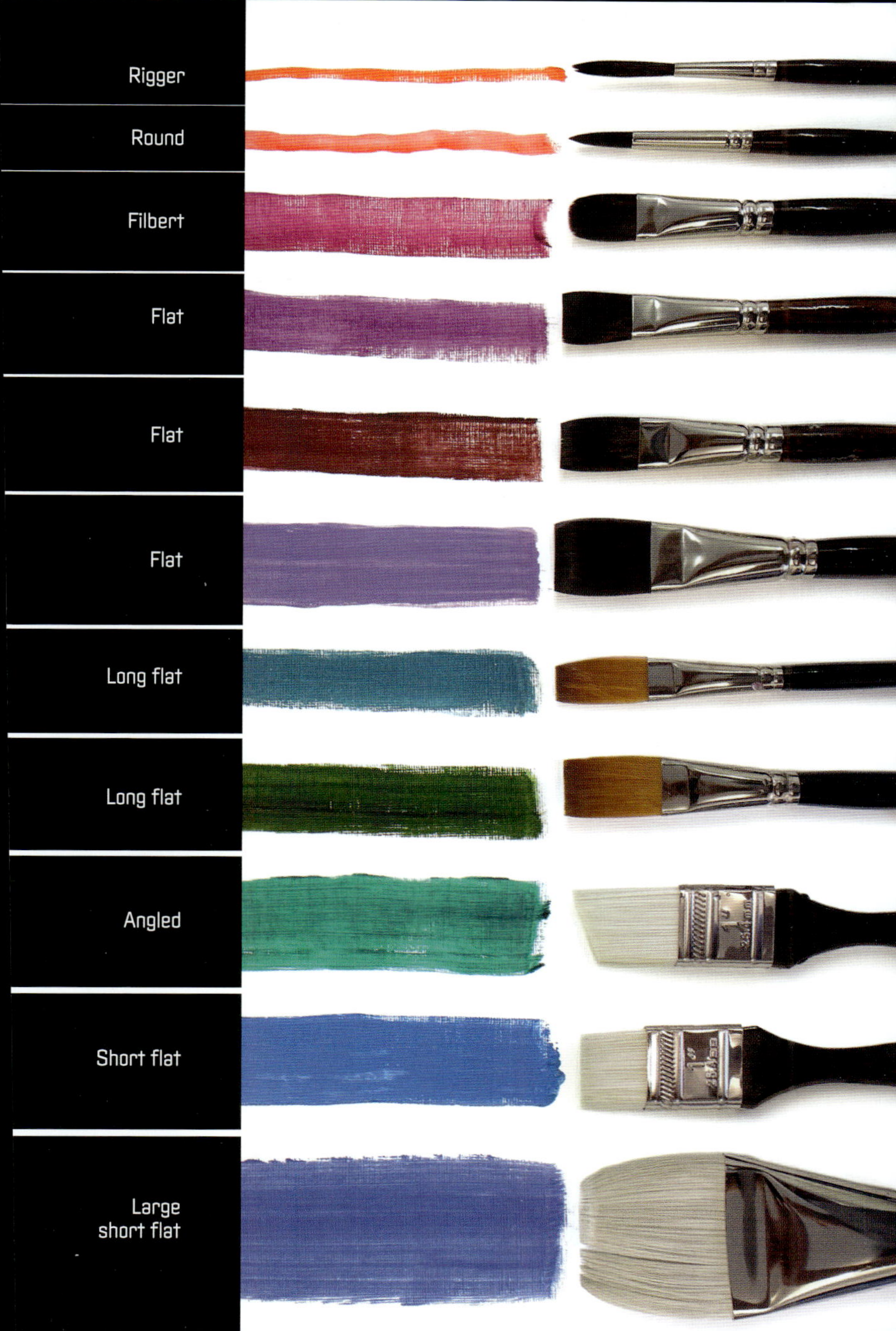

Rigger
Round
Filbert
Flat
Flat
Flat
Long flat
Long flat
Angled
Short flat
Large
short flat

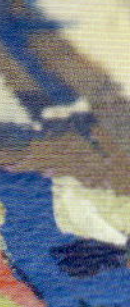

Which brush?

The brushes you need will depend on the marks you want to make – and therefore on what you're painting. For a beginner a maximum of six brushes would be adequate: two large, two mediums and two small, with a mixture of flat and round heads. If you prefer fine, detailed paintings you will probably need more round heads, but for looser applications large flat heads are best.

WHAT SIZE TO CHOOSE?

The number on the side of a brush represents the length, width or thickness of the brush hairs, although as these aren't consistent between manufacturers, it's best to check the sizes in person if possible.

Although larger brushes might seem intimidating, they simply mean you can cover more ground with more paint. Save the smaller brushes for detailed work.

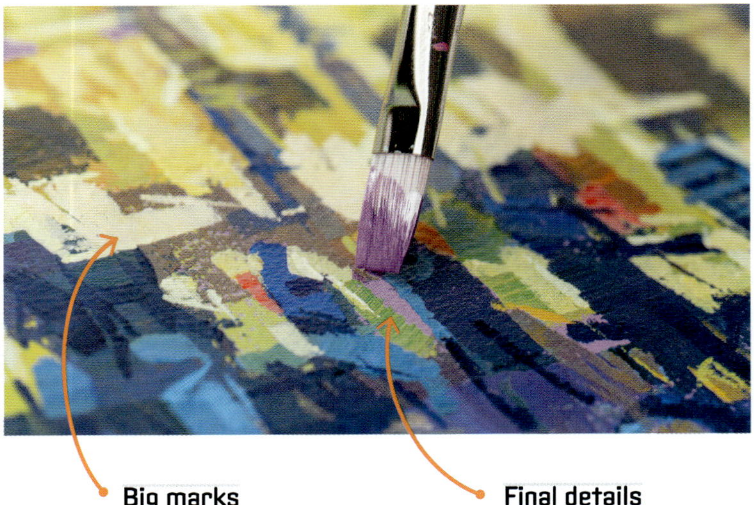

Big marks

A large flat brush, like the 37mm (1½in) flat used here, can make surprisingly fine lines, so don't be afraid to start big.

Final details

Fine lines can be applied in one stroke using a 12mm (½in) flat.

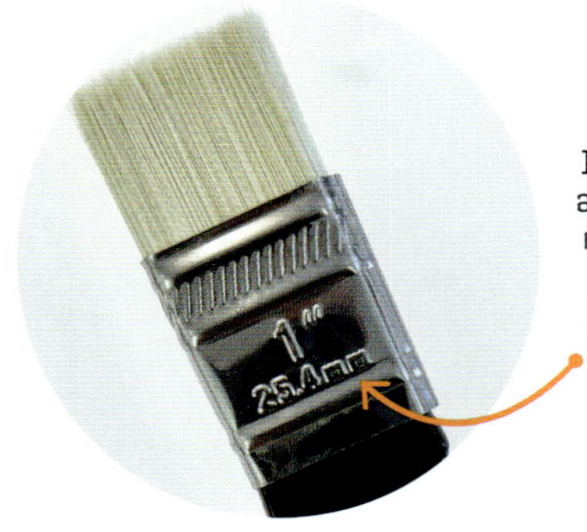

I use large-scale brushes which are more clearly defined by their numbers. These show the width of the brush head in inches, along with a metric conversion.

OTHER QUALITIES

Hair type Brushes are available with many different hair types, both natural (including sable, squirrel, hog and even goat) to synthetic man-made fibres. The qualities of the hairs affect the handling: firmer bristles allow more paint to flow, as it just glides off the brush. Some brushes are relatively soft but firm up when loaded with paint – this means that it's the pressure that you apply that determines how much paint is released.

Handle length The length of the handle is also a consideration. Longer handles allow for looser brush work while shorter ones are better for more precise work. There are even handleless brushes, which are designed to be gripped in your palm for freewheeling strokes.

Other applicators Some acrylic brushes don't even have bristles – instead they are solid angled block of rubber or, as in the example below, strips of flexible plastic.

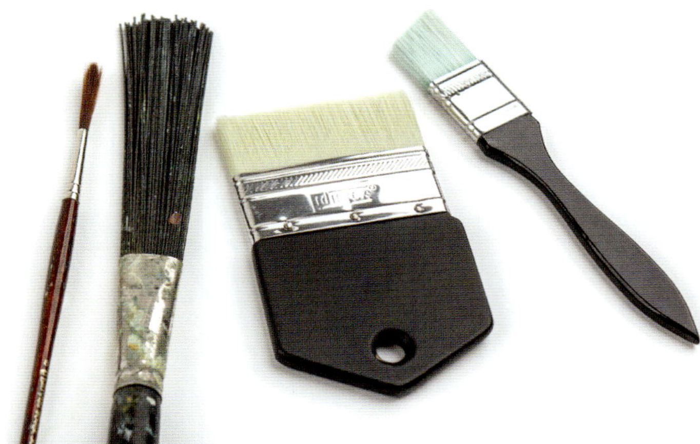

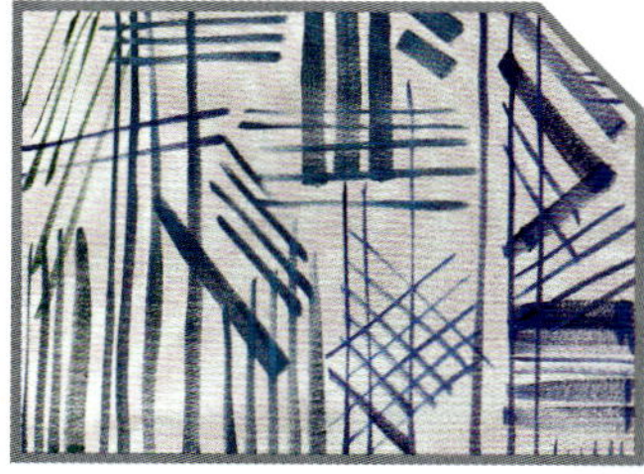

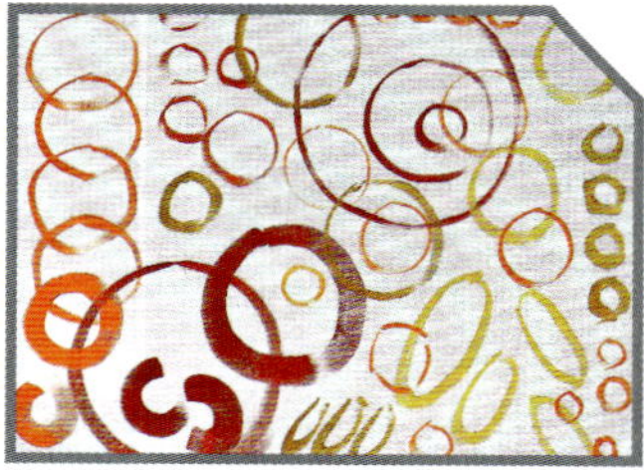

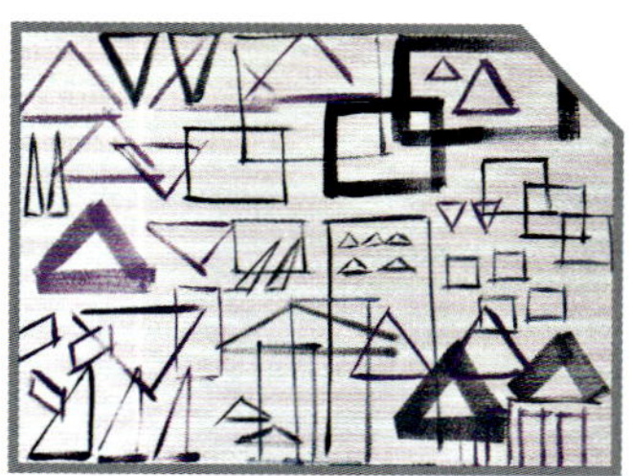

Warm ups

I really want to stress the importance of warming up before you invest time or resources in a painting. This is something I neglected when I first started out, as I was really keen to get going on a proper painting – but after years of spoiling perfectly good canvases and pristine sheets of watercolour paper, I've discovered even a ten-minute painting or drawing warm up does wonders to dispel tension or anxiety, and improves the actual painting considerably.

You really don't need to do anything dramatic – just a few scribbles or drags of paint to help loosen your painting arm.

Here are a few advantages of doing a warm up before you start:

- Doing a warm up helps to create momentum.

- It starts the creative engine and helps prepare you mentally to engage fully with your process.

- Confidence becomes paramount in painting and that requires a more relaxed attitude.

- Spoiling a few rough sheets of paper is fine; spoiling multiple canvases drains confidence.

GEOMETRIC

Renaissance artists would practise drawing circles and other geometric shapes to prepare. Try to draw a series of lines in quick succession, and see how straight you can get them; or draw small circles quickly and try to get them as round as possible.

Thumbnails

A little thumbnail of your artwork goes a long way in visualizing what's in your head, and will help to take away any apprehensions you might have over spoiling your support. See page 86 for more on thumbnails.

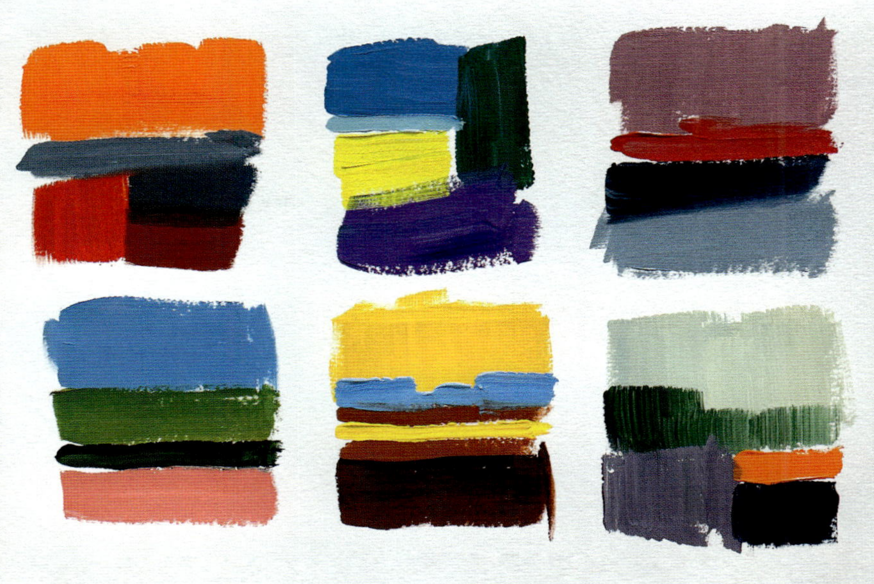

Mix up some colours to create a swatch of the colours you're thinking of using for your artwork.

STRETCH, DON'T FLEX

Be careful that your fun warming-up sessions don't become too
extended – or you'll be painted out before you get started.
Restrict the time you spend and don't become too precious over
these exercises – you can show off in the real painting!

Preparing your paints

Acrylics paints are water-based, so they can be thinned down with nothing more than tap water. You can also clean your brushes simply by rinsing them. Alternatively, acrylics can be diluted using various specialist mediums including flow improver (see page 32), matt or gloss medium and even retarding fluid (see page 34). You can also use water and these additives in combination.

Whatever you use will affect the way the paint behaves. Using water will dull the richness of the pigment and, as acrylics dry rapidly, you'll get some uneven drying times. This makes blending a little tricky. Using flow improver, either diluted with some water or neat, works very well in maintaining the strength of pigment.

Paint consistency

Diluted paint takes longer to dry than paint straight from the tube. How long you have to work – and how it will behave – depends on the amount of water you add to the paint.

DILUTING YOUR PAINTS

Squeeze the paint into a palette well, use a brush to add water, then gently stir until you get to the consistency you want.

It's worth practising creating different consistencies by varying the proportions of paint to water.

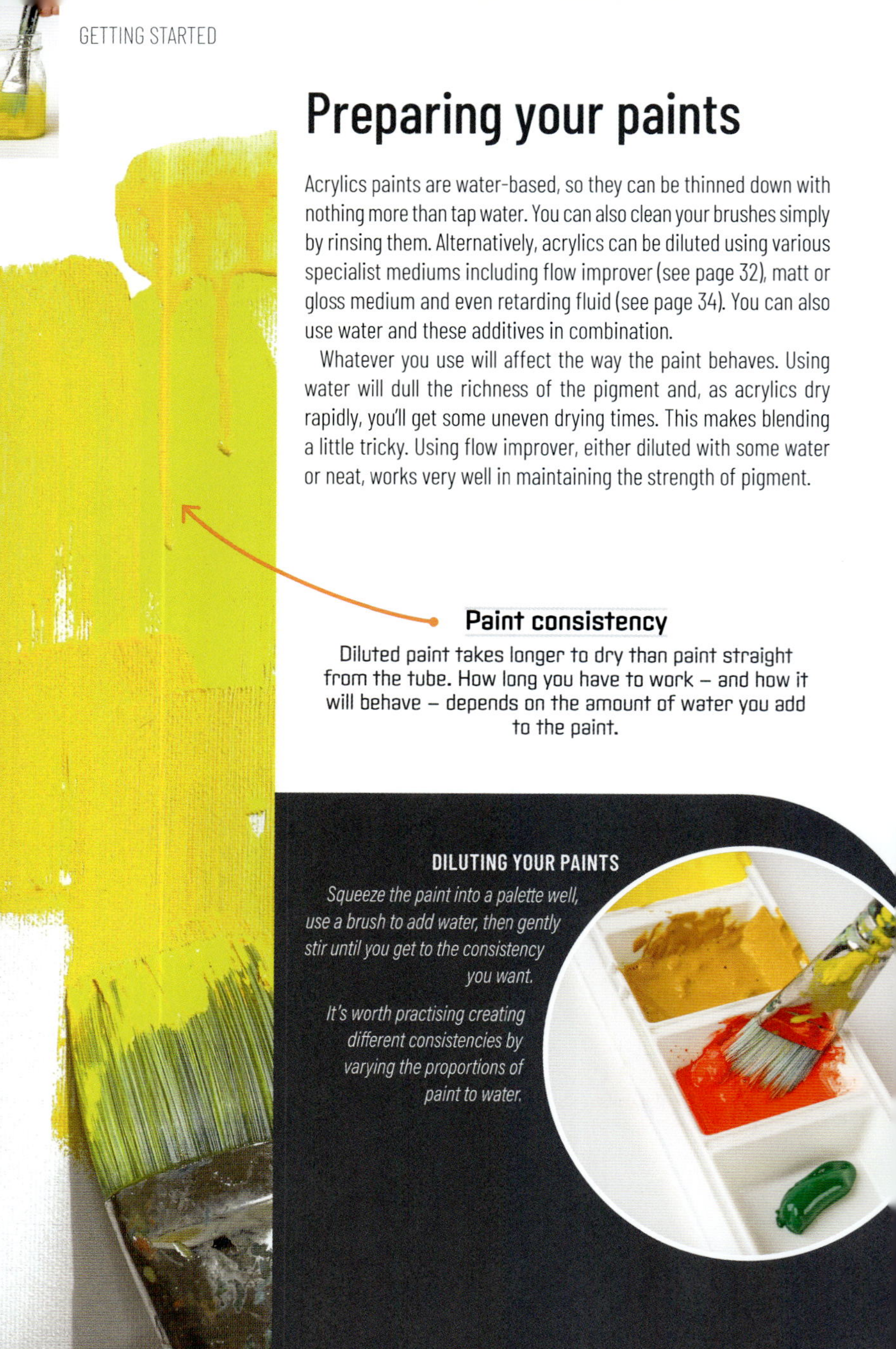

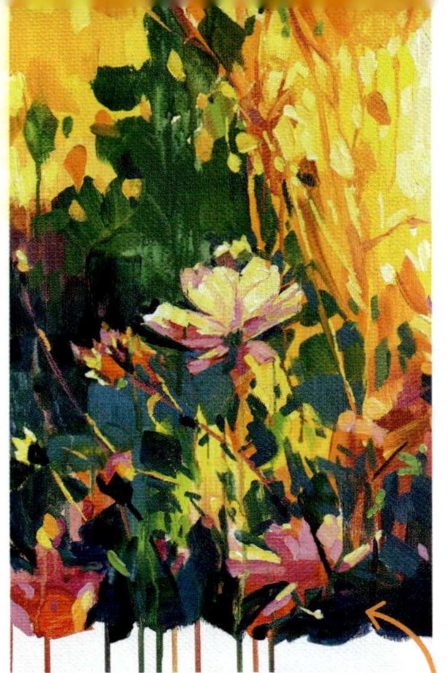

Acrylics lack the subtlety of watercolours but give you potency and variety through use of thinner and thicker applications.

THE WATERCOLOUR STYLE

You can create effective results by diluting acrylics to a watery consistency and using them for washes and other watercolour techniques.

This example shows the advantages of using acrylic in a watercolour style. Rather than colouring in a drawing you can improvise by going in directly with diluted washes to draw upon subtle blends and running paint.

Once the initial colour has been introduced and allowed to dry, you can use darker tones or thicker paint to shape the various elements.

SURFACES FOR THE WATERCOLOUR APPROACH

Cartridge paper Thin paper will warp and buckle: use a thicker grade of paper or stretch paper on board.

Watercolour paper This will absorb the diluted paint, creating more authentic watercolour effects.

Primed watercolour paper Laying down a base of diluted white acrylic paint before you start will seal the paper, like a primer. Painting over this will result in streaks from your brushstrokes, but the paint will glide more smoothly over the surface. Colours appear brighter, but where paint is very diluted, excess pigment will create pools of uneven colour.

Diluted paint on untreated watercolour paper.

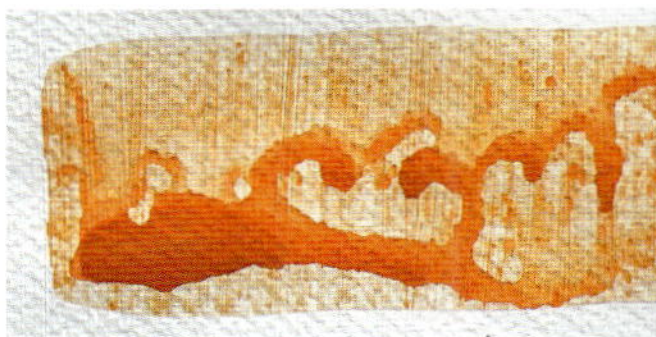

Diluted paint on primed watercolour paper.

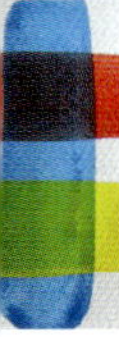

Glazing

Glazes are transparent layers of thin paint built up one after the other to help create depth and can also unify a painting. The technique of glazing is extremely popular with watercolourist and can work well with acrylics, too.

WHY ACRYLICS?

Because they remain watersoluble, watercolour washes can be reactivated and reworked by adding water. This makes each layer less stable than acrylics.

The advantage to using acrylics for glazing is that they are waterproof once dry and cannot be reworked, making glazing extremely reliable.

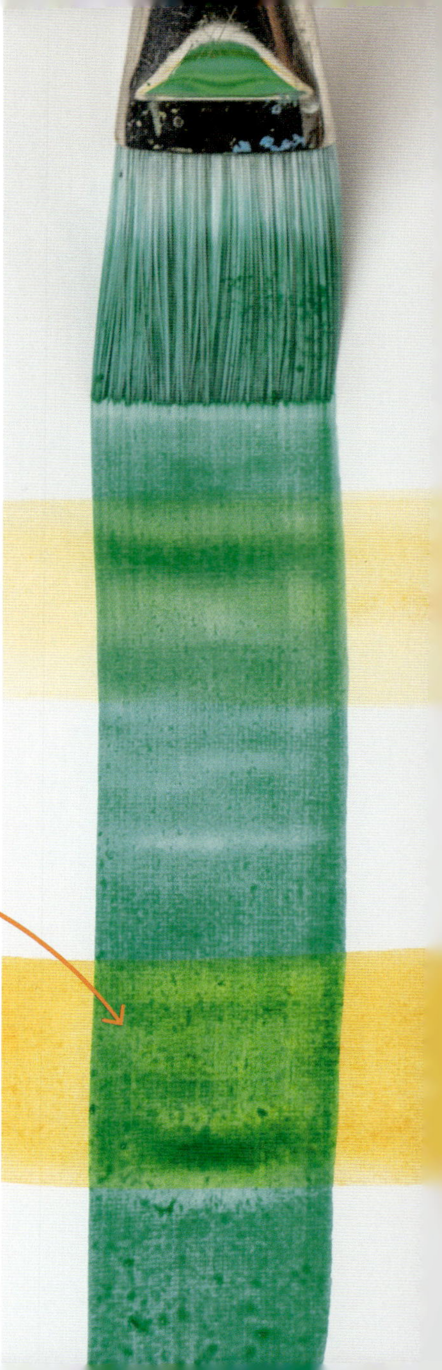

When glazing, the paint is diluted to a strength that means the dry underlying layers remain partially visible, creating a mixed colour.

Open acrylics

If you want to work back into paint, there's an acrylic paint for that: a type of acrylics called 'Open Acrylics', which allows you to reactivate earlier applications – a little like watercolours.

GLAZING PRACTICE

STAGE 1 Apply a thin layer of orange diluted with water to prime (see page 21) acrylic paper. This creates a ground colour and tone.

STAGE 2 Once dry, sketch out the tube of paint, then use a similar thin wash to define the subject. You'll notice the colour and tone go darker when placed on the first dried layer. Allow this layer to dry.

STAGE 3 Colours and tones can be modified with each new layer. Use diluted violet to pull the darker tones forward. Once these have dried, apply less diluted orange to heighten some mid-tones. Add small amounts of white mixed with orange to create subtle highlights.

Limit the number of layers to retain freshness – too many glazes will result in muddy shades.

STAGE 4 Once thoroughly dry, paint a glaze of diluted orange over the entire artwork. This adds a orange film over the violets to unite the painting while adding more depth to the image.

STAGE 5 Use neat paint to contrast the subtle glazes: white for the rich lights and pastel orange for mid-tints. Finally, apply neat violet to optimize the darks.

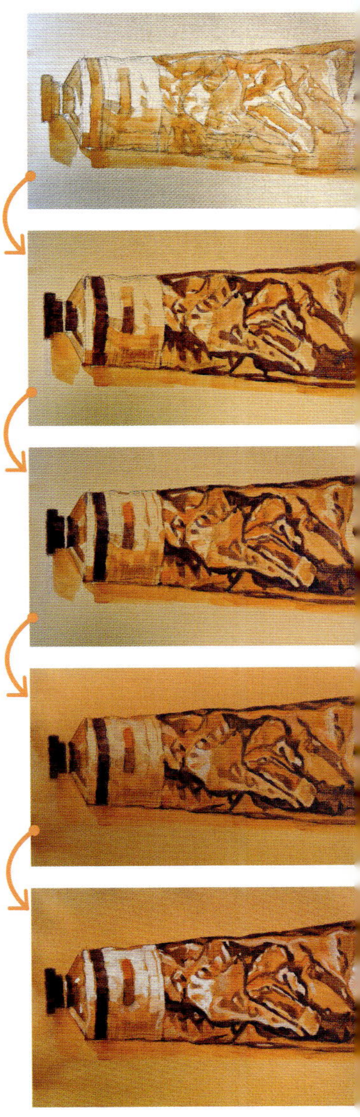

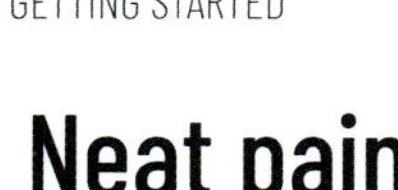

Neat paint

Working with neat acrylics means using the pigment almost completely undiluted. Instead of laying several thin applications one on top of another (as in traditional painting techniques), you apply one thick layer. If you're covering a wide area, you apply one thick layer next to another and build up the scene like a mosaic. Some layers may be thinner for contrast. Once these layers are dry you simply add the finishing touches.

WHY USE NEAT PAINT?

- Acrylics are most vivid and luminous when used straight from the tube or pot.

- Artworks are completed more swiftly. Building up thin layers takes time – and leads to monotonous brushstrokes that rob the painting of energy.

- Using neat paint encourages economy of brushstrokes, and energizes a painting as each mark looks vital and unfettered. You're less likely to overwork the piece.

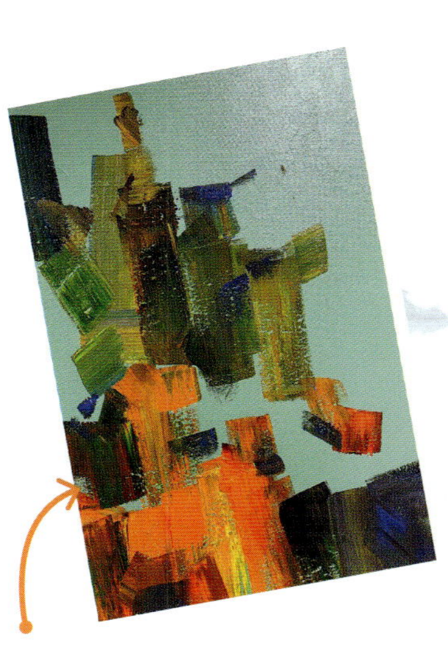

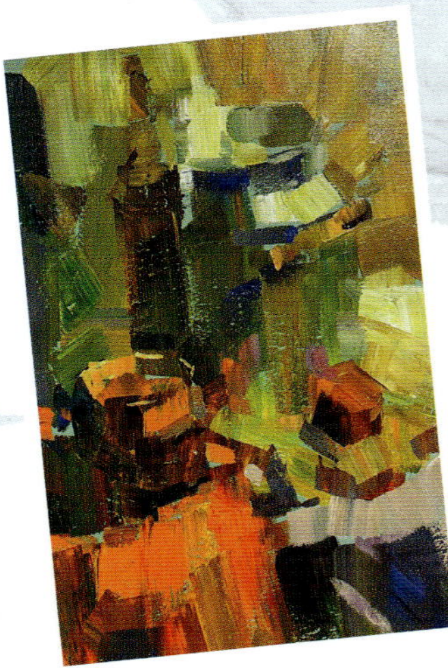

BUILDING UP

Here's an example of a still life using applications of neat, heavy-bodied acrylic paint. Brushstrokes are applied and left with no fuss, then another layer added next to it. Once everything is implied, the final lights, darks and refinements are included.

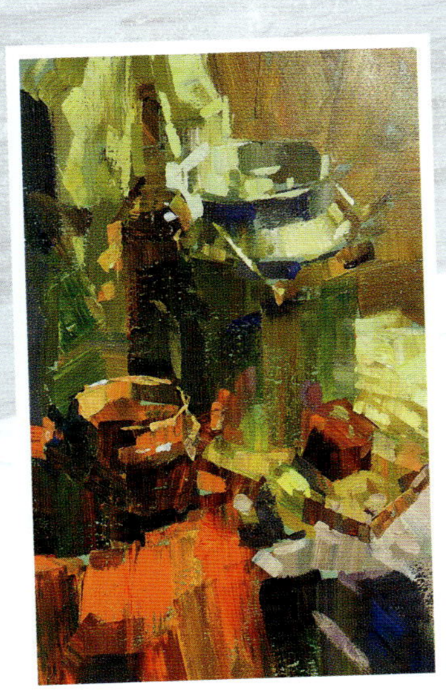

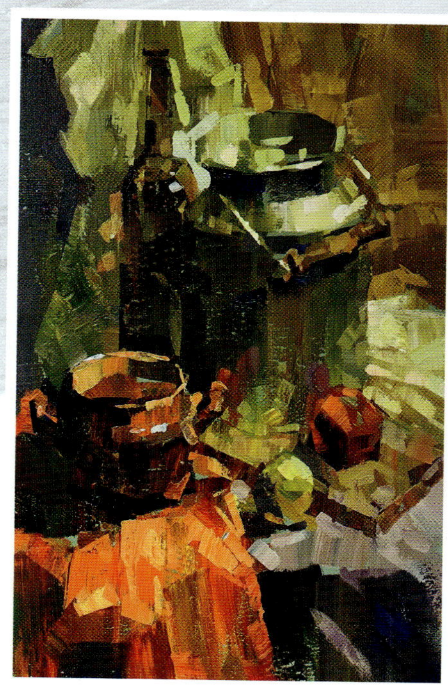

NOTES AND FURTHER IDEAS

Don't be puritan The purpose of using neat paint is to keep results fresh, not to restrict yourself – so feel free to you use water sparingly where it helps. I use a little water to dilute acrylics for base colours, for example, while during painting I'll moisten the brush before loading paint to avoid the pigment drying on the bristles.

Smooth flow Remember that acrylics are water-based: any overworking or watering down the paint will diminish the strength of colour.

Add body You can buy heavy body acrylic paint or add modelling or texture paste to soft body acrylic for extra bulk.

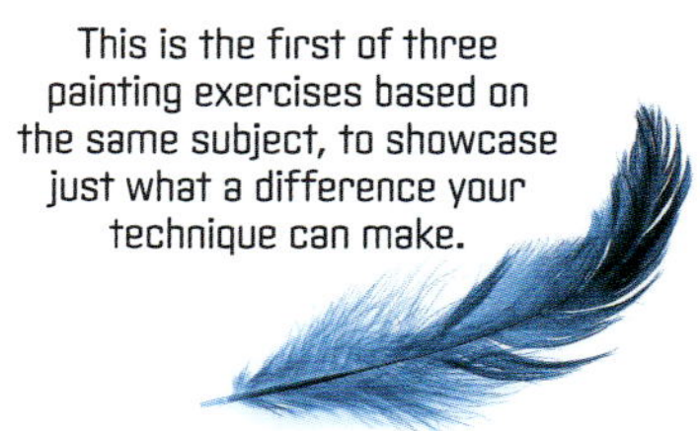

This is the first of three
painting exercises based on
the same subject, to showcase
just what a difference your
technique can make.

Following a drawing

Paint a parrot #1

This is a straightforward approach to painting a parrot: draw it out and colour it in. The colours simply follow the outline of the drawing, so you can be precise with the layers, and concentrate on getting the mixes right.

Start by sketching out the parrot on acrylic paper, then dampen a medium-sized flat brush, and use it to begin to apply various shades of red and orange to the parrot's head. Once complete, move on to the next area of colour, and repeat until the parrot is painted.

Swap to a clean brush (or thoroughly rinse the same one) for each new colour to ensure crisp, distinct marks and clean colours.

FOLIAGE TIPS

Mid and lighter greens A variety of greens is important. White, plenty of yellow and small amounts of blue will create bright greens. Using less yellow creates mid-greens. I also use pure sap green for cleaner greens.

Dark greens Mix deep violet with sap green to create darks, and apply them sparingly. Add a tiny shot of white into the dark mixes to soften them for variety, and blues and greens for the shadows in the background. You can afford to loosen up – go for bigger shapes and avoid painting individual leaves.

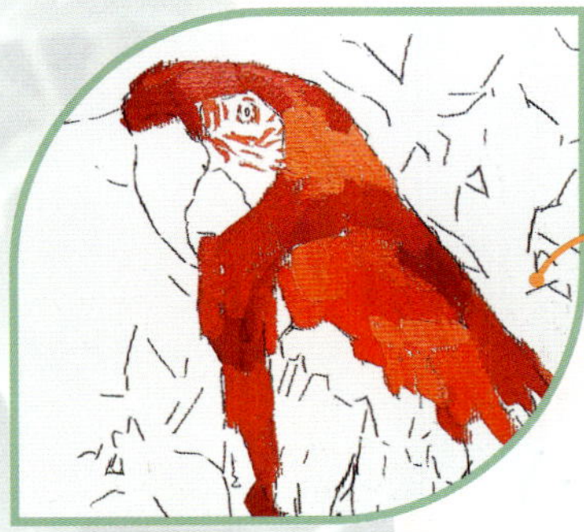

RED HEAD As you work, vary the tones of each colour to ensure a vivid, striking effect.

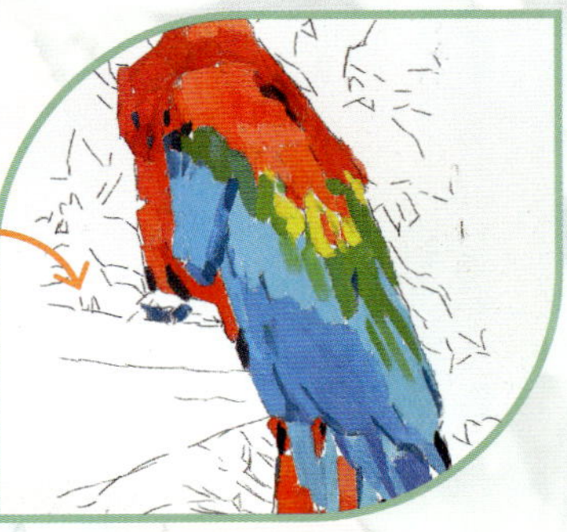

VARYING COLOURS AND TONES
For the blues, add white to soften them; or a small amount of violet for the darker shades. A medium yellow is used for the yellow marks.

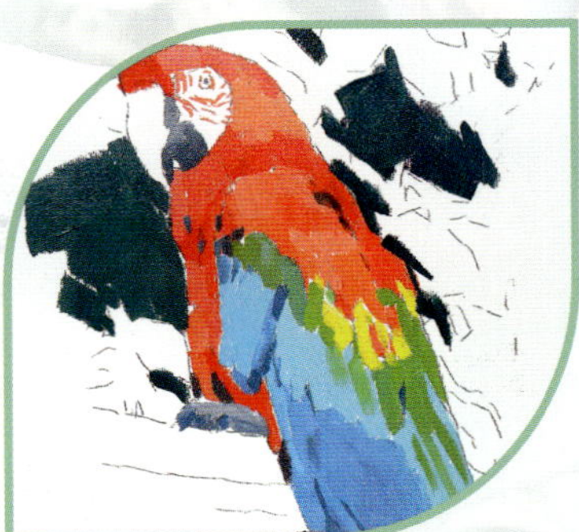

FOLIAGE AND PERCH Keep your colours clean by keeping sections harmonious, with little colour interaction. Use a neutral dark to help draw features out.

THE FINISHED PARROT

For the parrot's platform, use a mix of the lighter greens, with a dab of red to vary it. Use the same colour with more white for the beak. Introduce strong darks at the end to define the shapes.

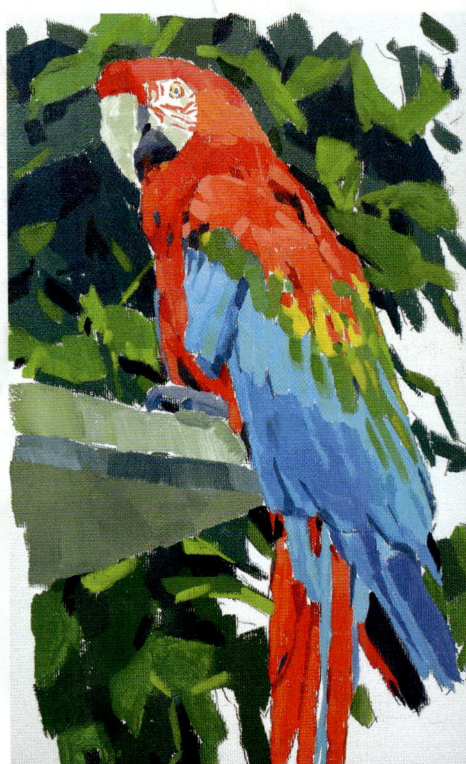

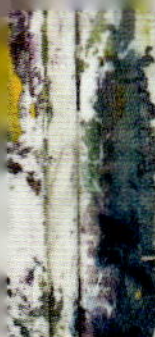

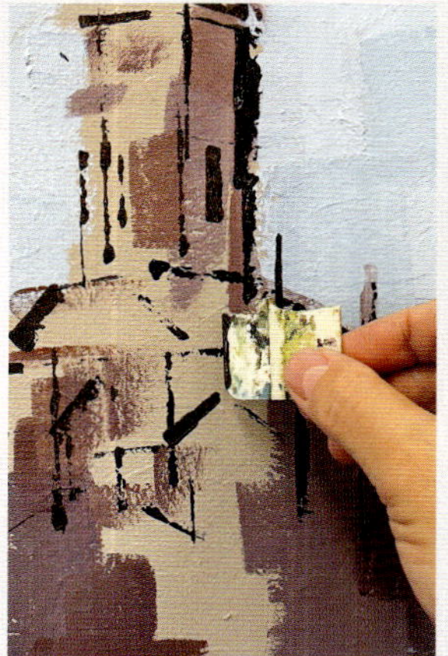

Linework with a card

Too much drawing in your artwork makes it look overworked or fussy. This leads to unwanted focal points that can draw undue attention to weak drawing skills.

Using small plastic squeegees to draw with will give concise edges that have a lovely textural quality, which varies with the pressure applied. This detail from a larger street scene showcases the variety of linework this tool makes available. I started without a drawing, instead blocking in the big shapes using a large flat brush and limited palette.

Once you are ready to add the linework, mix black and white to create tonal variations. Prepare large quantities of the mixes in a range of tones on your mixing tray using a brush. Use the edge of the squeegee card to scoop up some dark colour and apply it as shown above left.

TIPS

- Try to make a decisive mark in one go.

- You can twist the card a little to produce different marks, or vary the pressure for thinner or thicker lines.

- Circular edges can be squared off, or a smaller card can be used to create a rounded shape.

- The card will need a little wipe after one or two applications to keep the lines concise – just use a tissue to clean it, then simply reload and carry on.

- If any lines aren't quite right, you can mop them away with a damp tissue.

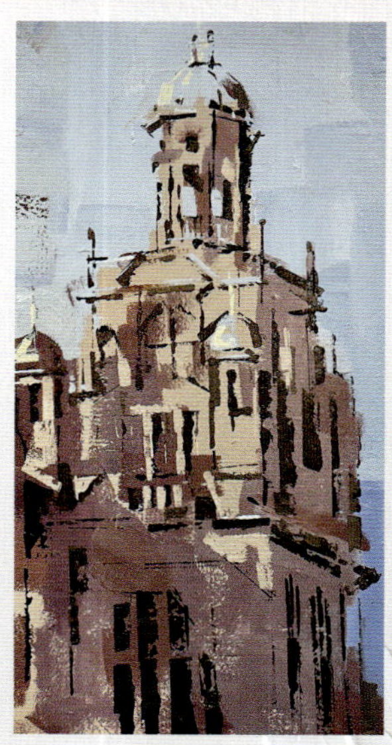

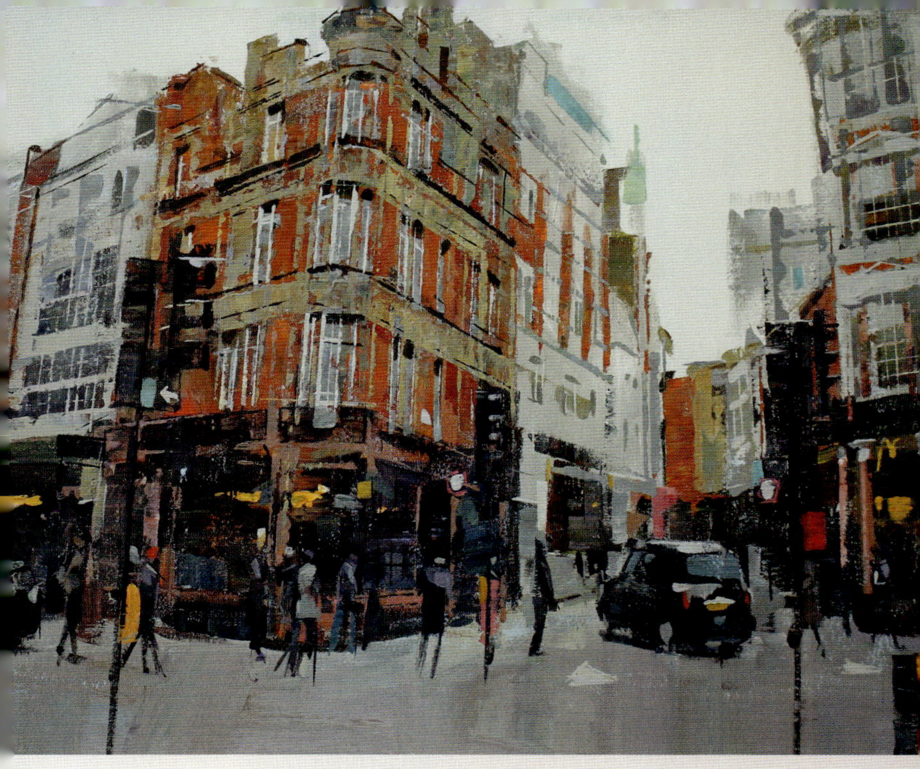

SQUEEGEES AND MORE

*I bought a variety of these squeegee cards online
and used a large pair of scissors to cut down a few to
make smaller sizes. They're as useful for laying down
large areas as they are for linework.*

*You can achieve similar effects using palette knives,
old loyalty cards or thin pieces of card.*

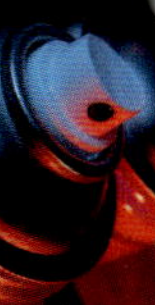

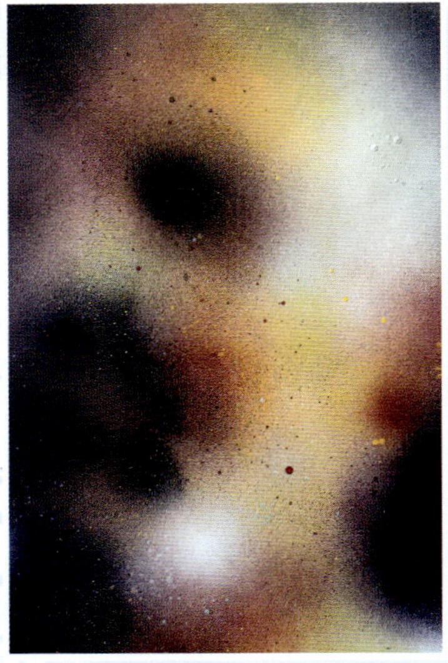

BLURRY FACE

This shows acrylic spray paint without any additional after-painting. Once the main shapes are in, the artwork can be developed using other acrylic techniques.

No initial drawing was used here: spray can be unpredictable, so I judged the placement of facial features by eye.

Spray!

Try combining acrylic spray paint with traditional heavy body acrylics. There are a few brands of acrylic spray paint with an incredible range of bright and subtle colours.

The spray can be focused in a small area or used as a fine mist, depending on the spray cap you choose. This helps to creates subtle blends that are difficult to achieve using traditional acrylics.

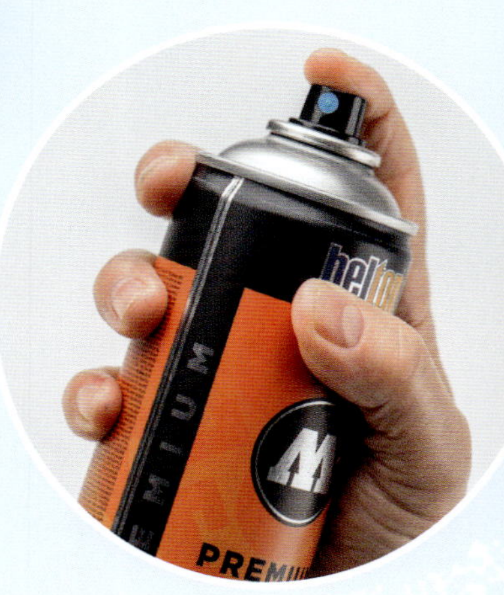

Play safe Use spray cans outdoors or in a well-ventilated room. Wear a face mask.

Sharp finish Run magic tape around all four borders – once you finish, peel it away to reveal clean, sharp edges.

Avoid clogs When spray cans clog, they spit out irregular patterns. Avoid this by occasionally shaking the can, tipping it upside down and spraying for a few seconds to clear the cap.

FRENCH BULLDOG

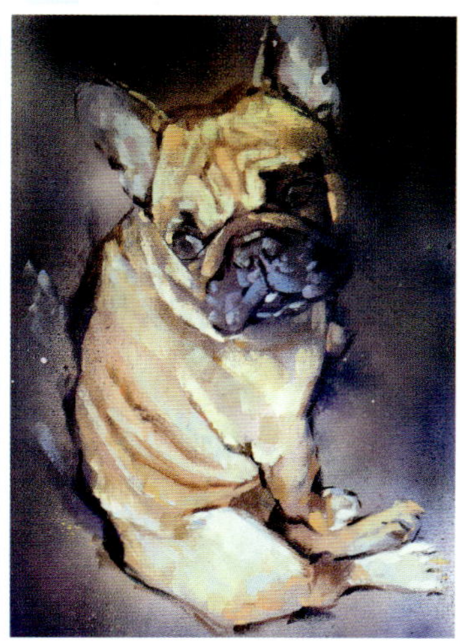

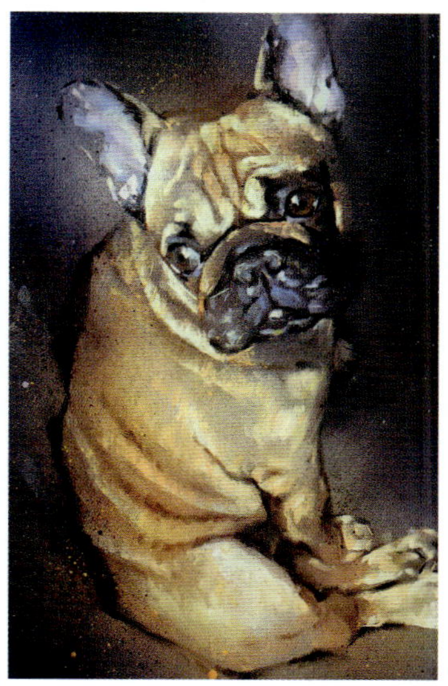

STAGE 1 Use spray paint to create a blurry image of the dog on acrylic paper with yellows, orange and ochre for the dog, and combinations of blues, purples and blacks for the background and shadows. Once the spray has dried, swap to acrylic paint and brushes to block in the features.

STAGE 2 Add more intense colour with the spray cans – they will meld seamlessly into the painted areas. Allow to dry, then intensify the painting with fairly neat acrylic paint, using smaller flat brushes for controlled strokes and strong highlights. You can use a larger spray can nozzle for a couple of larger blobs – as shown below.

Vary the distance of the spray from the surface ranging from long-distance fine mist for soft blends to closer, more focused applications for intense colour.

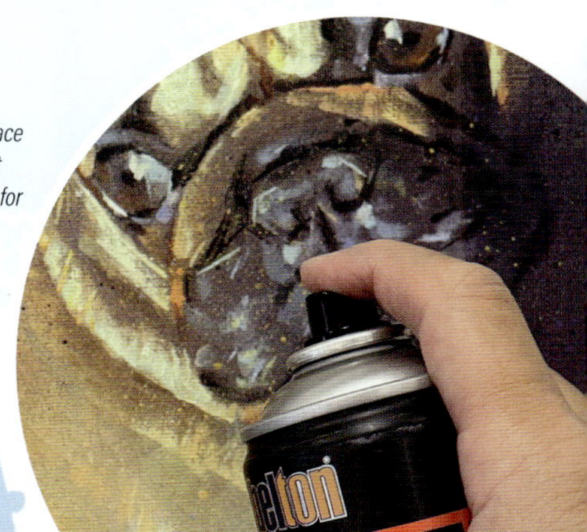

Mediums: flow improver

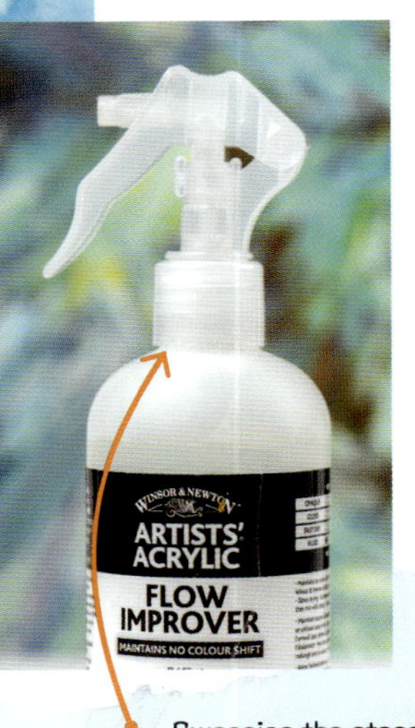

A clear liquid medium that generally comes in bottles, flow improver is something I have used a lot and would recommend, especially if you are interested in blending and using the paint thinly. It is an acrylic medium (see opposite) that is used to dilute pigment in order to create washes, applications of flat colour or to improve the ability to blend.

In this way, it works just like water – but, as you can see opposite, flow improver helps to reduce brushmarks and keep things smooth. As acrylics come in such a variety of consistencies you may instead opt for the paint type that suits your painting process.

Swapping the standard lid for a spray nozzle lets you spritz it evenly over a painting.

WHERE TO START WITH FLOW IMPROVER

If you have not used flow improver before, start by using it mixed with paint in small areas.

- Try diluting paint for your backgrounds with water, but employ flow improver for the main foreground elements to see the difference.

- Acrylic colour can dull when mixed with large amounts of water. Flow improver allows paint to be diluted while still retaining colour strength.

- Flow improver can be used alongside water in different proportions. When used neat, it will leave an almost satin finish.

- When using flow improver, drying times will be slightly extended in comparison to using water. How much longer you have to work will depend on how much flow improver you have used.

FLOW IMPROVER COMPARISON

Paint diluted with water on the left; and diluted with flow improver on the right.

WHAT IS A MEDIUM?

Flow improver is an example of an additive medium – a catch-all term for substances added to acrylic paint that change the consistency or qualities of the paint. Mediums (we use this term to distinguish them from painting media) often come in paste, gel or liquid form, which are added to your paint. Note that using a large proportion of these mediums with paint can diminish colour.

You can buy mediums that change the gloss of the finish, the texture, drying time or other qualities of the paint. In fact, the sheer range of additives and enhancers you can use with paint can be overwhelming. Some are more useful than others. I recommend flow improver, retarder and perhaps modelling paste, but others can be gimmicky. They should also be used sparingly. It's tempting to absolutely drench a painting with masking fluid, creating unwanted and unnatural cut-outs to be filled with pale tints or left as highlights, but with experience you will learn that it's more effective to use one or two spots of masking fluid for a specific effect.

While mediums can be useful, they are no substitute for what will really enhance your painting: simple practice. Ultimately, all you really need is paint and water to clean your brushes or to dilute paint for greater coverage or blending.

Slow things down

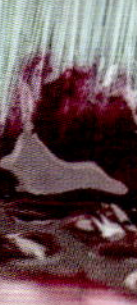

The rapid drying time of acrylic paint is both a blessing and a curse. While very thick applications can take hours to dry, thin layers will dry in minutes – sometimes more quickly than you'd like. To extend drying times, you can use acrylic retarder: a small amount added to paint will prolong working times.

Unlike adding water or flow improver, retarder does not affect the consistency too much, allowing you to retain the texture.

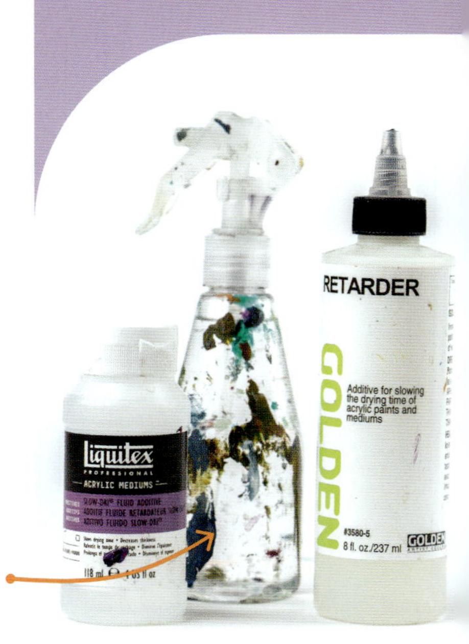

Retarder is perfect for giving more time to blend the colours in a large sky or when you want soft graduations of tones in a portrait.

DIFFERENT TYPES

Retarder is available in liquid or gel form.

Gel retarder It is important to use gel retarder in the correct proportions (see opposite). Using too much gel will dull colours and change the qualities of the paint.

Liquid retarder This can be dispensed into a spray bottle and sprayed onto wet paint on the surface, allowing time to blend. Use liquid retarder at the start of a painting when you need to cover large areas quickly and need some of the colours to mix.

Fresh paint

Retarder can be sprayed on your mixing tray to help keep colours fresh. This is invaluable if the mixes are very complex, or spread thinly over the palette when painting outdoors.

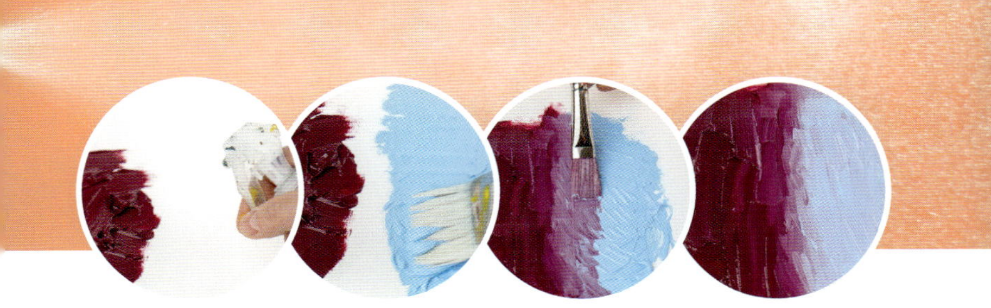

SPRAYING FOR SUCCESS

Using retarder makes blending colours seamlessly into one another easier.

STAGE 1 Apply a layer of paint to your surface, then use a diffuser bottle to spray retarder evenly over the initial layer.

STAGE 2 Apply a second paint next to the first.

STAGE 3 Gently work the two paints into one another at the point they meet. More blending will make the transition smoother – so if you want to retain the texture, don't overwork it.

TICK TICK TICK

Paint quickly and – more importantly – decisively. Retarder does not provide the huge working times familiar to oil painters. It does, however, give you a vital few minutes, so make the most of them.

CHANGE IN TEXTURE, CHANGE IN TONE

Be careful not to over-use retarder – particularly the gel type – as this will overwhelm paint and dull colour. The mix can become tacky: always use a greater proportion of paint to retarder.

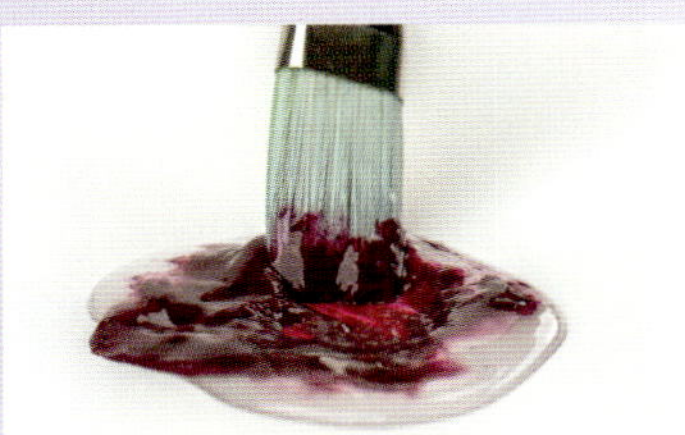

TOO LITTLE PAINT

Using equal parts of medium to paint will result in the paint splitting in the mix, the texture becoming noticeably tacky, and dulling the paint colour.

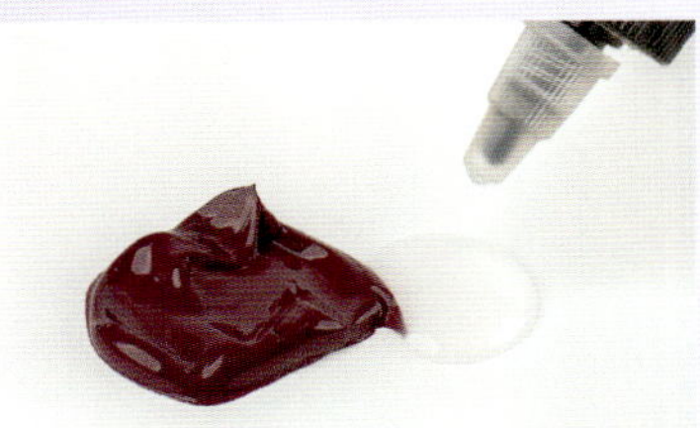

THE RIGHT AMOUNT

This proportion will give you vital minutes of blending time without adversely affecting the quality of the paint – or the finish.

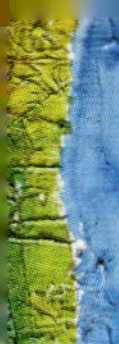

Modelling paste

Texture gels and pastes add structure for impasto brush marks or other effects. They can be added to acrylic paint or used on their own to create a base layer. As with most other acrylic mediums, avoid overloading the paint: colours will dull if you use too great a proportion of medium to paint.

- There are quite a few variations and thicknesses available. The names vary but all give broadly similar results.

- Modelling paste or structure gel is particularly dramatic when applied to your canvas before painting.

- You can embed elements into the paste such as pieces of card, paper or small objects like shells, dried flowers or old rope for collage effects. Once dried this makes your work appear tactile and contrasting against traditional painting methods.

- You can add the paste to paint for extra density so your brushwork has dramatic peaks and troughs.

- If you're using a soft body consistency of paint, modelling paste will add volume. You will notice some shrinkage to the impasto marks once it dries.

- Try mixing modelling paste into acrylic paint and work directly on the surface. Avoid blending; just apply marks of varying sizes side by side, perhaps making up a portrait. The extra dimension helps to creates a lovely contouring effect.

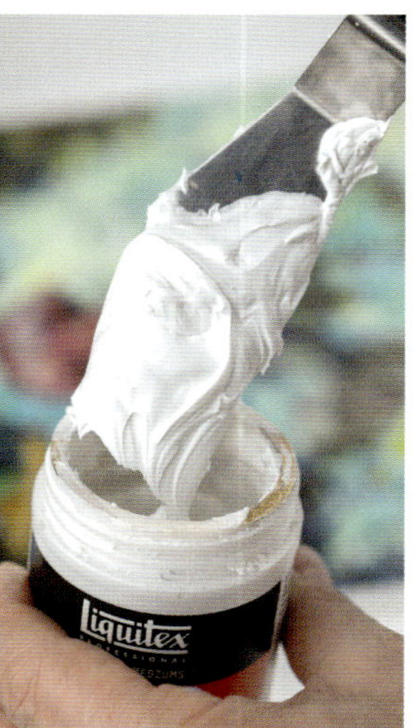

You can use a brush to apply the paste, or your fingers, or – as here – a palette knife.

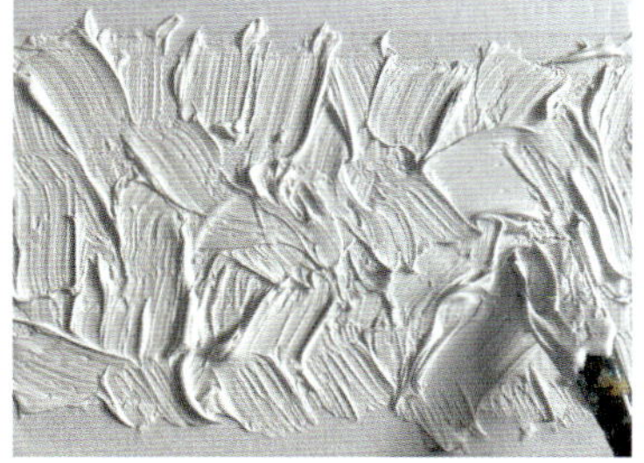

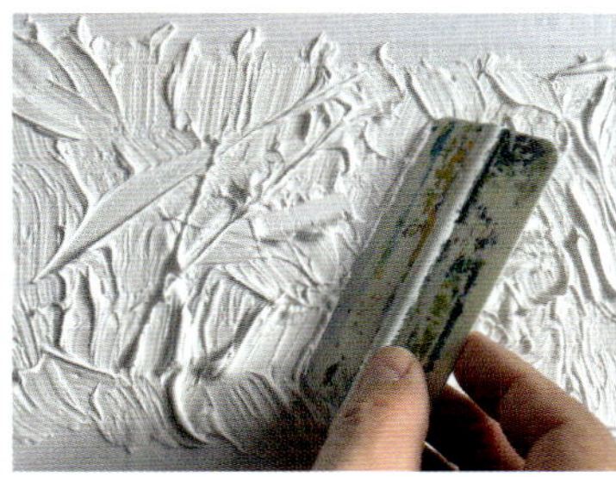

Running a layer of paint over the dried surface will show you how interesting the distressed markings are.

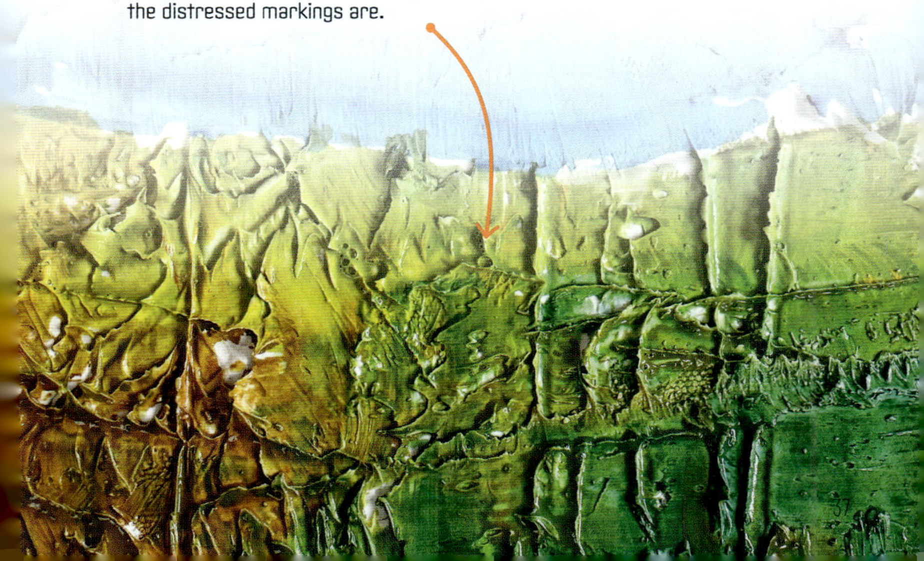

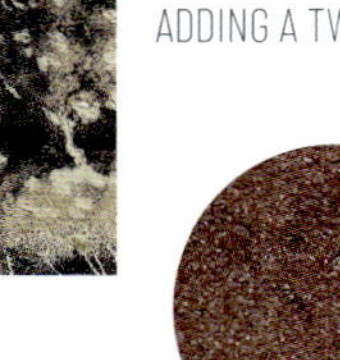

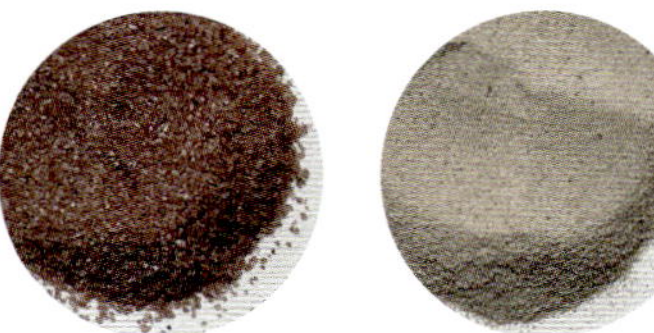

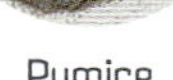
Crushed garnet

Pumice

Black flakes hex

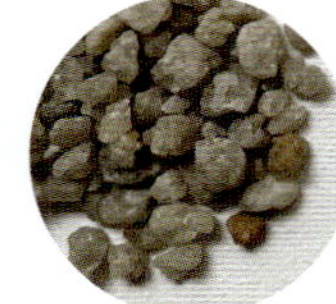
Gravel

Dry mediums

Usually bought in jars, dry mediums are inert particles, either natural minerals or manmade, with no binding agent. Some dry mediums, such as ground marble, can be used to thicken acrylic paint, though their main use is for creating textural effects.

I find dry mediums work best when placed on layers of wet acrylic paint: this showcases the surface value of the medium, such as the shine on black flakes or glass beads.

Alternatively, you can mix these particles into clear wet medium, which can then be used to create an extra layer of texture that can be painted over once dry.

Dry mediums work less well when mixed directly with acrylic paint, although even here they are useful for creating textures.

Whichever approach you try, be warned – the particles can get everywhere, so lay down plenty of protection.

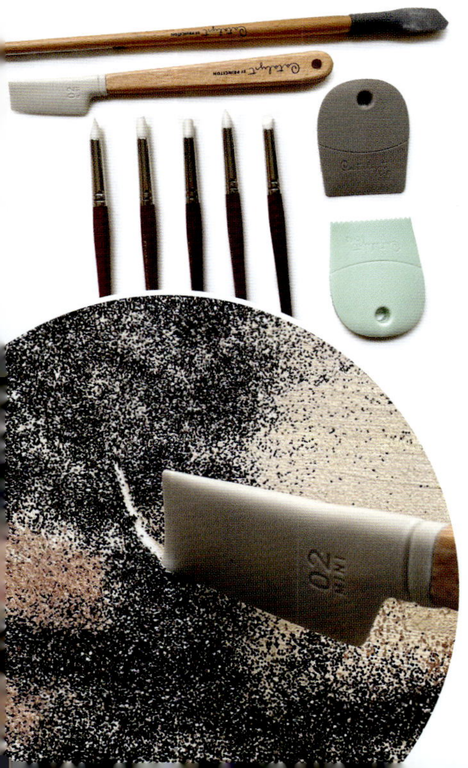

APPLICATORS

Silicone-tipped tools like those shown here can be used for painting, and are excellent for applying acrylic mediums – dry or wet. Try using them to score or blend paint; or for moulding mediums into interesting shapes and textures.

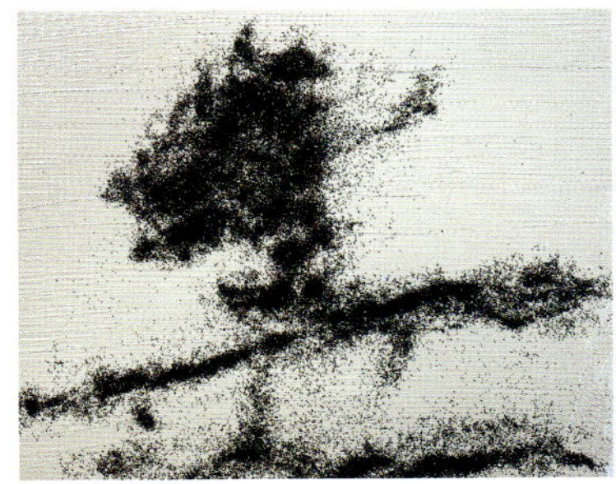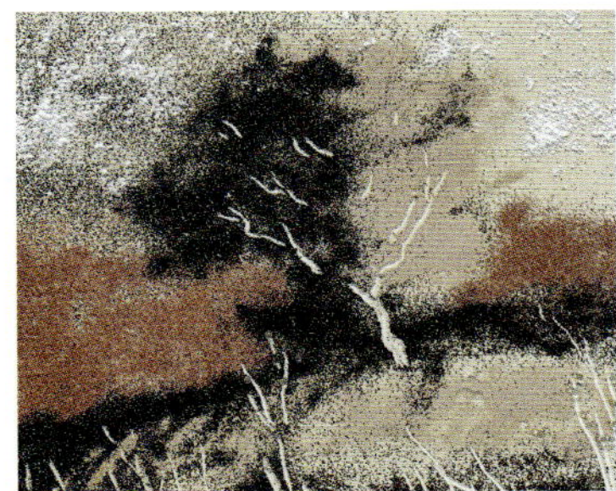

DRY MEDIUM LANDSCAPE

Try this simple landscape using dry mediums on a layer of thick, wet acrylic paint.

STAGE 1 Apply thick buff titanium acrylic to canvas paper, then sprinkle black flakes over the acrylic to form the shaded areas of the landscape.

STAGE 2 Sprinkle pumice in the light areas and crushed garnet for the background, then use a carving tool to score some branches into the tree.

STAGE 3 Add more buff acrylic paint in certain areas to allow more dry medium to be sprinkled.

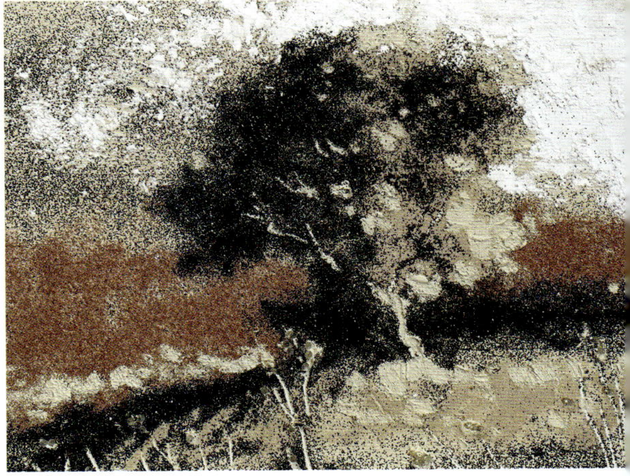

At the final stage of this painting, I included glass beads in the foreground and applied more ground marble to lighten the sky.

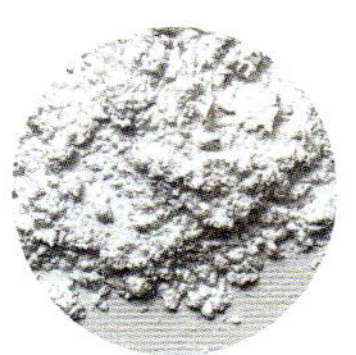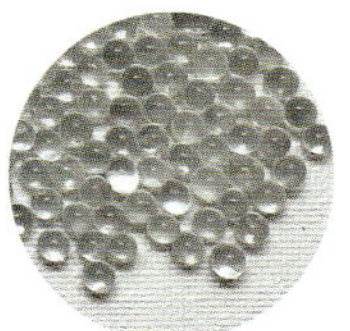

Ground marble   Glass beads

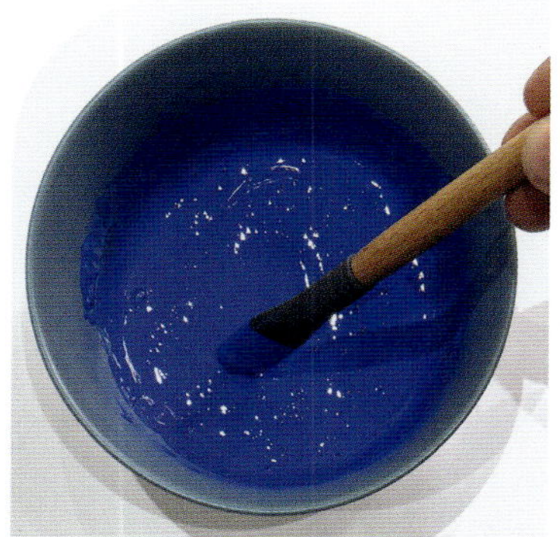

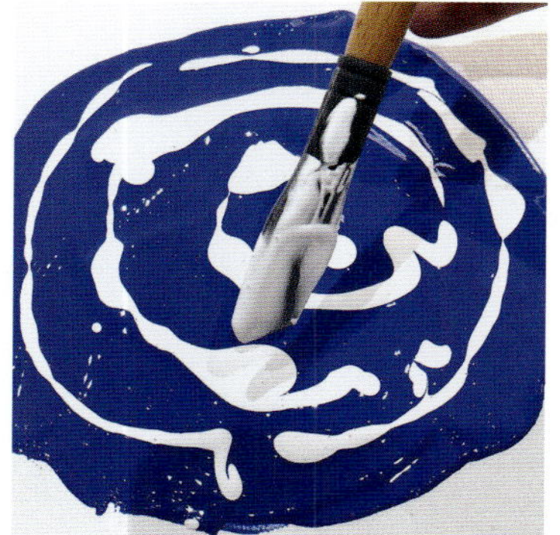

Colour pouring

Colour pouring medium has become very popular in recent years. This medium increases the flow of the paint without diluting or affecting the colour, which opens up pouring techniques.

To use it, you combine the medium with paint in a container (a bowl is fine) and stir them thoroughly together, as shown top left.

You then simply pour the paint directly onto the surface. In the example to the left, I poured a circle of blue onto acrylic paper, then added streams of white paint, also prepared with colour pouring medium.

The result is paint that keeps its form, creating interesting flows of colours and shapes. Critically, it won't crack as it dries, and the medium helps to ensure a smooth, even finish.

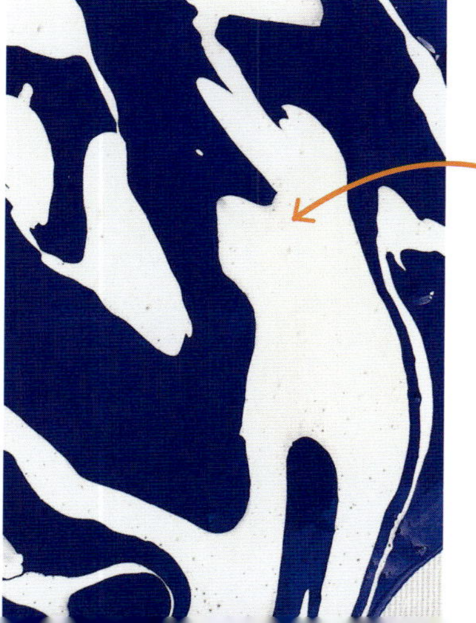

Tilt the paper to find other shapes – or try incorporating other colours.

Other mediums

Whether gel, paste or liquid based, when added to acrylic paint mediums will alter the translucency, flow, weight – or create special effects like iridescent or metallic finishes. None are essential but all provide interesting options. If you want to explore further, try some of the suggestions below.

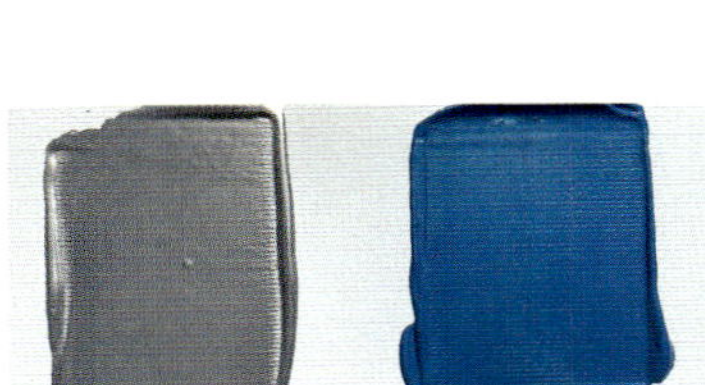

SILVER METALLIC MEDIUM

This creates a metallic version of any colour you mix it with. Adding metallic paint will give a glossier finish.

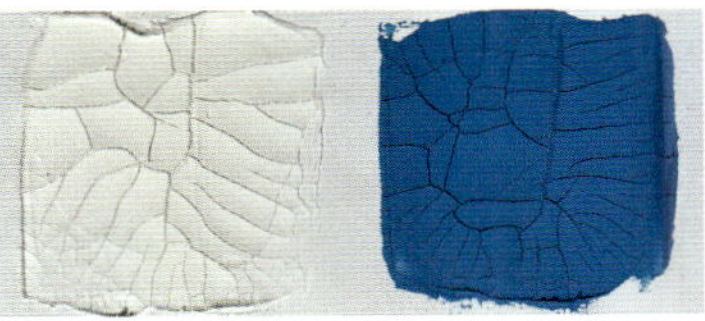

CRACKLE PASTE

Applied neat to your support or added to pigment, this causes your paint to crackle as it dries. The thickness applied will vary the effect: more paste results in wider cracks, while a thinner layer gives more closely-packed cracks.

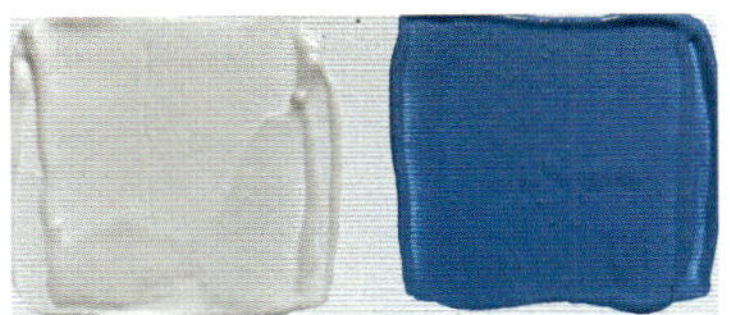

IRIDESCENT MEDIUM

This adds a lovely shimmer to colours. It's subtle compared to the metallic medium.

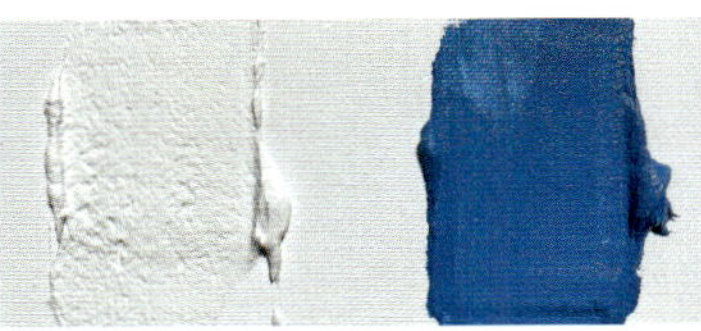

FIBRE PASTE

This can be used independently to add an interesting paper weave texture to the base of your paintings or mixed in with paint.

Pressure

The pressure you apply to the brush when painting can make a huge difference to the look of your artworks. As well as their use in creating an image, the marks you make will reflect your touch, confidence and emotion. If you're happy, the strokes will be freer and more expressive. If you're nervous, the marks will be tight and cautious.

Plant the seed early that paintings are a visual language and the brushstrokes used are a expression of how you feel.

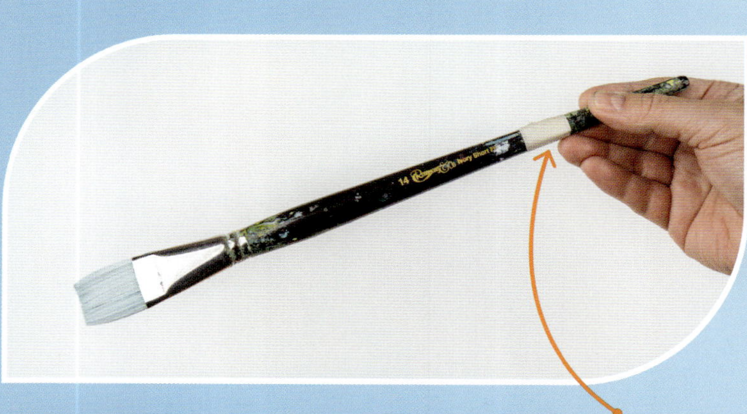

ALTER YOUR HOLD

Holding a brush like a pen or pencil may feel reassuring – but nearly all applications made this way will be tense. Conversely, being too relaxed means the paint will be applied with a complete lack of control.

Maintain a sense of discipline with the brush, whether tensed or relaxed. Try holding the brush further back from the bristles for more flexibility in the pressure you can apply.

In the throes of the painting it's easy to revert to the pencil hold. Wrap a little masking tape a short distance from the end of the brush to remind yourself where to grip.

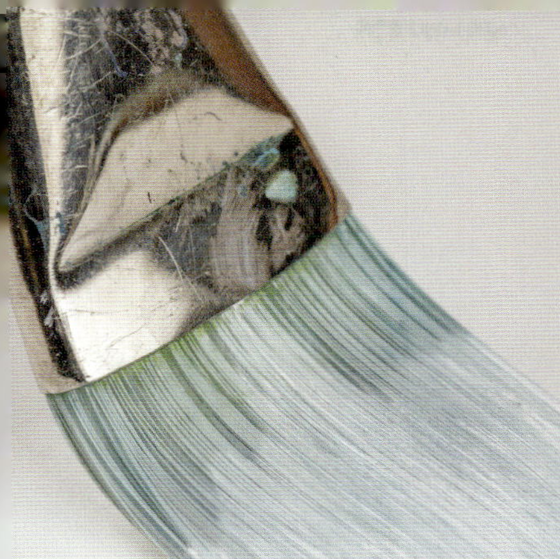

USE BIG BRUSHES

Large brushes help to develop confidence: the sheer size forces you to vary the pressure you use if you want to alter the mark you make. Over time you'll develop greater dexterity with larger brushes, giving a greater range of options – whereas a small brush will only ever make a certain sort of mark. Start the big brush work in the backgrounds or in large areas and work towards smaller brushes.

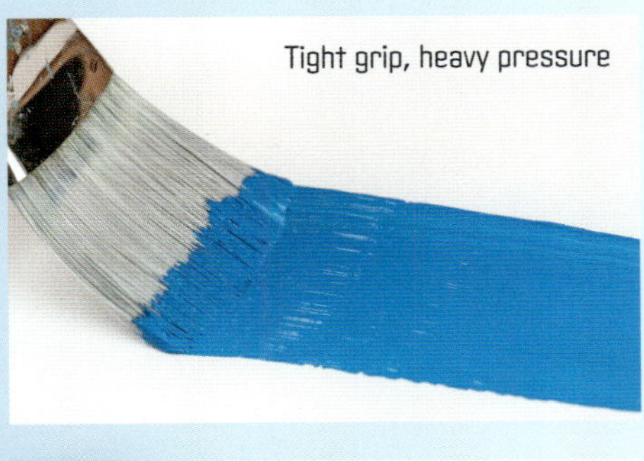

VARIETY OF PRESSURE

You can make interesting marks simply by varying the pressure you apply to the brush: just compare the flat, clean look of the marks made when the brush is wielded with a tight grip and heavier pressure, with the broken, varied marks made when the brush is held with a loose grip and lighter pressure.

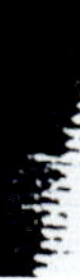

Beyond pressure

Pressure, of course, is only one part of the equation – the marks below show some of the range of marks available to you simply from one brush: in this example, a 25mm (1in) short flat.

Curves

Made with constant even pressure, the eye will calmly follow a curved stroke like this, creating a relaxed, safe feel.

Repetition

Steady, monotonous marks are good for anchoring shapes.

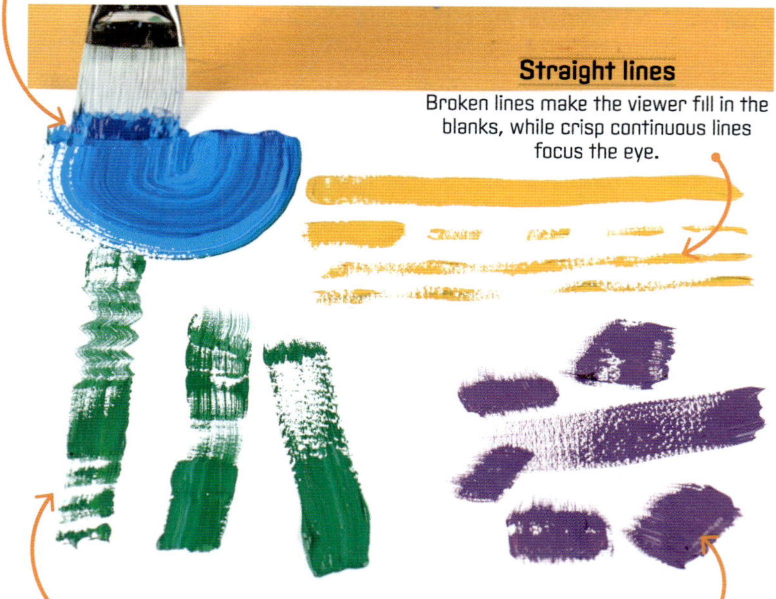

Straight lines

Broken lines make the viewer fill in the blanks, while crisp continuous lines focus the eye.

Twist, turn and wave

Break up regular shapes by twisting, turning and wavering the brush while varying the pressure from light to firm.

Granular marks

Jabs and flicks made with firm pressure create great contrast against solid applications.

COMBINATIONS

There are infinite marks you can make – and that's before you bring in combinations of marks, colours and brushes. Shown here are some key ideas to think about when making marks – whatever your subject.

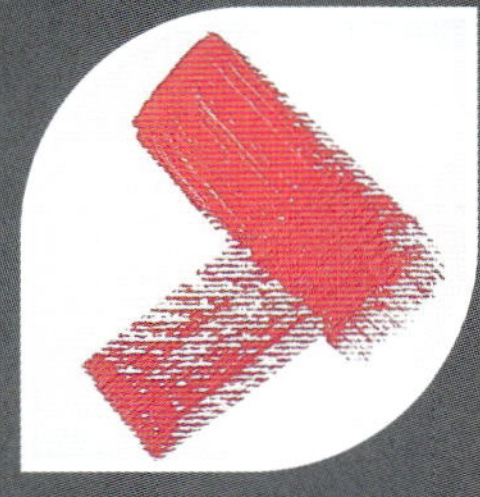

DIFFERENT ANGLES

Every brushstroke has to be made in a certain direction – so there is a decision to be made.

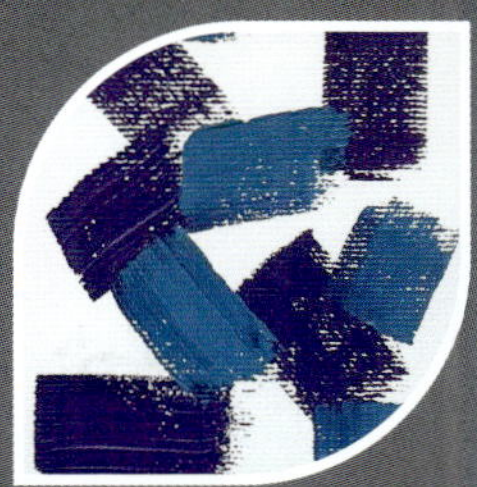

ANGLES AND COLOUR

Introducing more colours will add complexity and richness. Will the strokes you make with the new colour contrast with the others, or echo them?

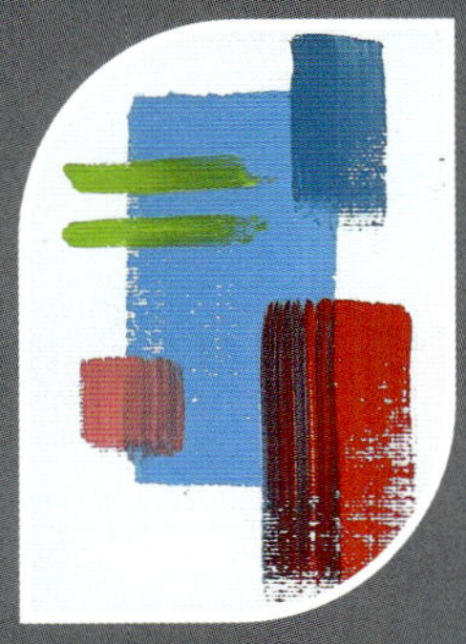

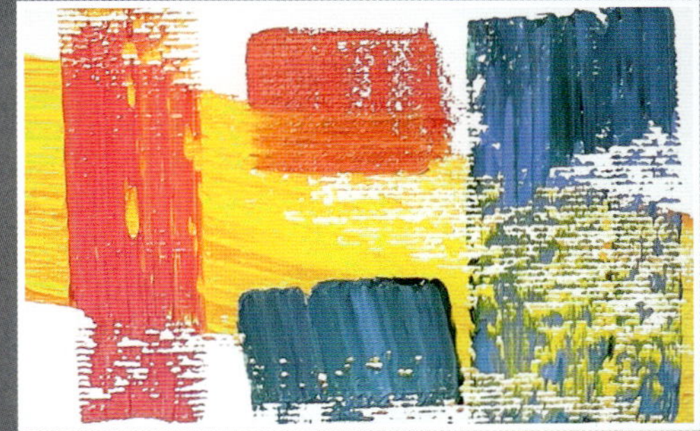

VARIATION

Even when all the marks are made in the same direction, you can create interest by using different size brushes, varying the length of the strokes, or overlaying the marks you make, as shown above left.

Once you bring in looser or tighter strokes, loading different colours on one brush and applying them in single strokes, and running colour over previous marks before they dry, you'll see there's a world of options just within abstract brushstrokes.

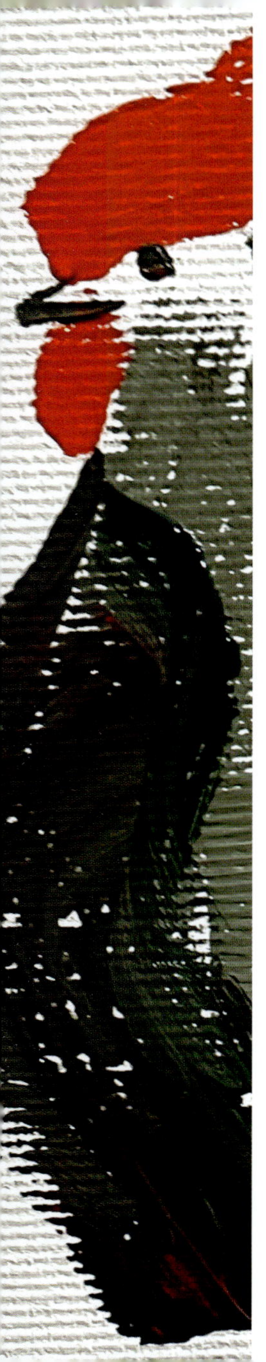

Make every mark count

It's easy to overwork a painting by building up excessive layers or adding details with dozens of brush marks. Multiple layers deaden colour and make your artwork look fussy – so be decisive and make every mark count when you're painting.

This exercise will help you retain the freshness of the paint – and your enthusiasm. Here I'm painting a cockerel, but the principle applies to any other subject. Even complicated scenes can be broken down into simpler shapes.

For this exercise, use just one brush – a medium flat head – and three paints: red, green and white.

> ## Economy of brushstrokes will help you get to the point and maintain the energy in your artwork.

STAGE 1 – NECK AND BODY Mix green and white, and begin. The first two marks form a triangular shape for the neck; a third mark establishes the top of the body, and a fourth the lower half. Ease off the pressure as you apply the latter strokes to create a little texture.

STAGE 2 – TAIL AND BREAST Using a darker mix, add three diagonal lines: one large and two small marks for the back feathers. Use a single broad rounded stroke for the chest, allowing the colours to streak a little.

STAGE 3 – HEAD Add a small bold stroke of pure red for the wattle, and a larger semi-triangular dab above the eye for the comb. Swap to the dark mix and finish be adding one tiny mark for the eye, a mini triangle for the beak and a line with a dent halfway for the leg.

NECK AND BODY

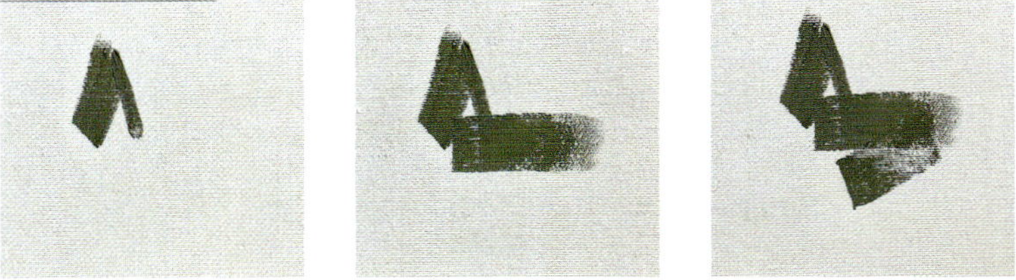

TAIL AND BREAST

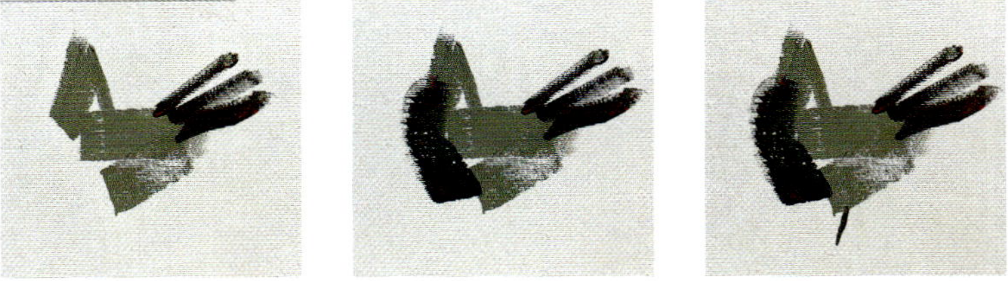

HEAD

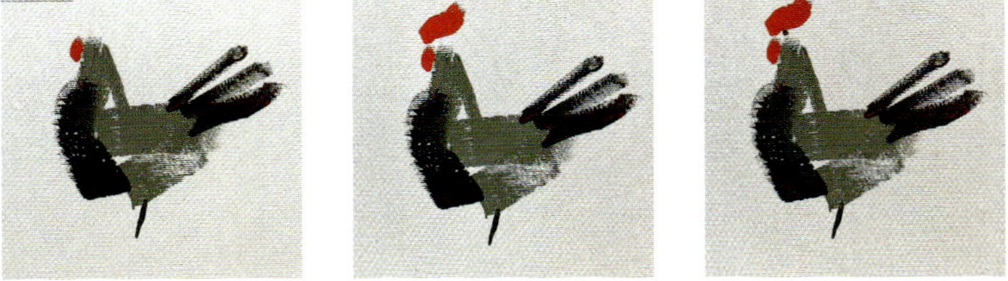

LIMIT YOURSELF

Once you've showcased the subject matter in its simplest form, you can elaborate with details knowing the essentials are there and everything else is a bonus.

Avoid overworking: set yourself a limit on the numbers of marks you make or time you spend on refinement.

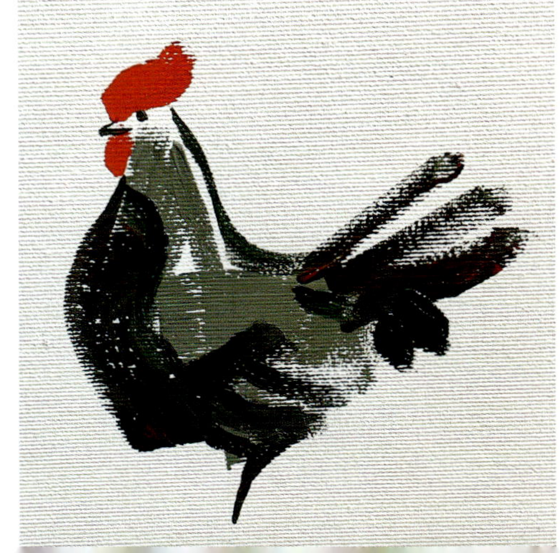

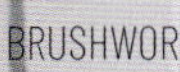

Drawing with a rigger

Beginners tend to hold brushes like pens or pencils, with all the pressure concentrated on the fingers. This can lead to very stilted linework. Using a rigger brush is a great tool to begin loosening up your drawing arm. Artists use these small, long-haired brushes for fine detail, such as adding rigging on boats – in fact, this task is where they get their name. The extended bristles provide a lovely spring when applying marks, unlike a short round brush, which can be too rigid. You can purchase various sizes; which you choose will depend on how fine you want the linework to be.

The long hairs hold lots of paint and release it slowly and evenly, giving smooth, clean lines.

Hold the rigger with a few fingers, in a relaxed grip. Work more from the wrist by pivoting the brush between your fingers.

A rigger brush is a round-headed brush with extended bristles that come to a fine point.

PICK THE RIGHT TYPE

Rigger brushes for watercolour usually use natural animal hair, as this sort of hair keeps its shape, gives spring to the painting action, carries lots of fluid paint and deposits it smoothly. As acrylic is a coarser medium, acrylic rigger brushes generally use manmade synthetic fibres that give a slightly stiffer feel and handle heavier, stickier paint better. The results, however, are very similar for this weightier type of paint.

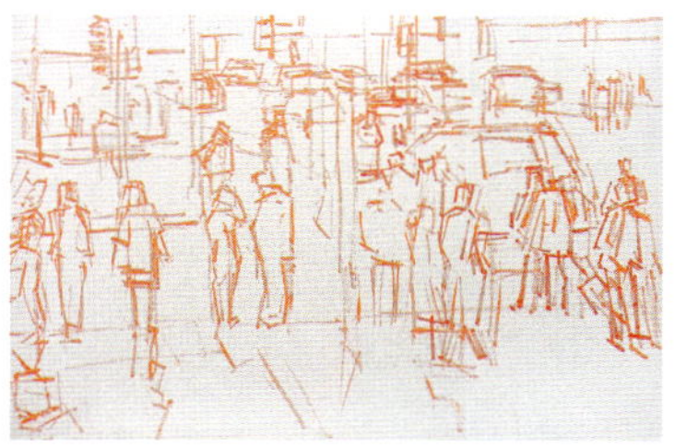

EARLY OUTLINES

I love drawing or laying an outline prior to painting using a rigger brush. As you can see from these examples, riggers are ideal for architectural paintings where both precision and a painterly feel is needed in the detail.

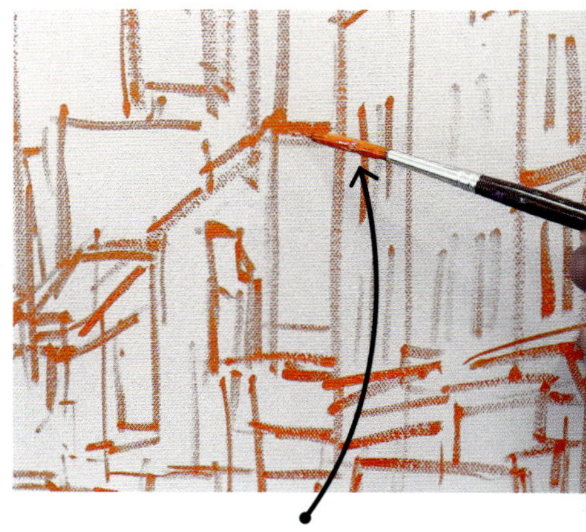

The extended brush head is less precise, but the variety of linework the brush has to offer as you build up a sketch more than makes up for it.

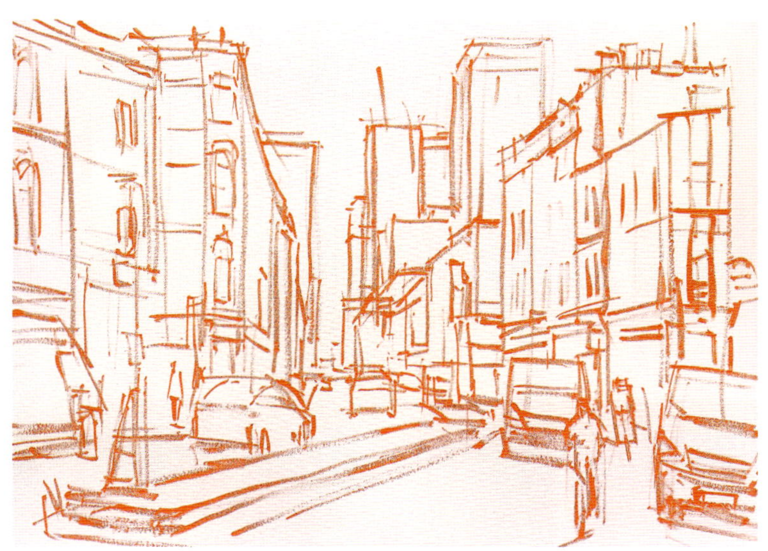

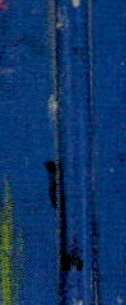

Outlines – the drawing lasso

This exercise is a great way to define shapes in your artwork. Edges in painting are often softened off or gradually fade into one another. You'll see this a lot in historical oil portraiture where smoky edges are common. In the nineteenth and twentieth centuries, art movements such as Impressionism and later Expressionism turned this tradition on its head, and began to use outlines to pull shapes forward and make the elements clearer.

Artists from the Expressionist movement in particular favoured very coarse thick lines with an almost geometric look – as in the piece below. It's a great technique that will allow you to grab the viewer's gaze and pull it where you want.

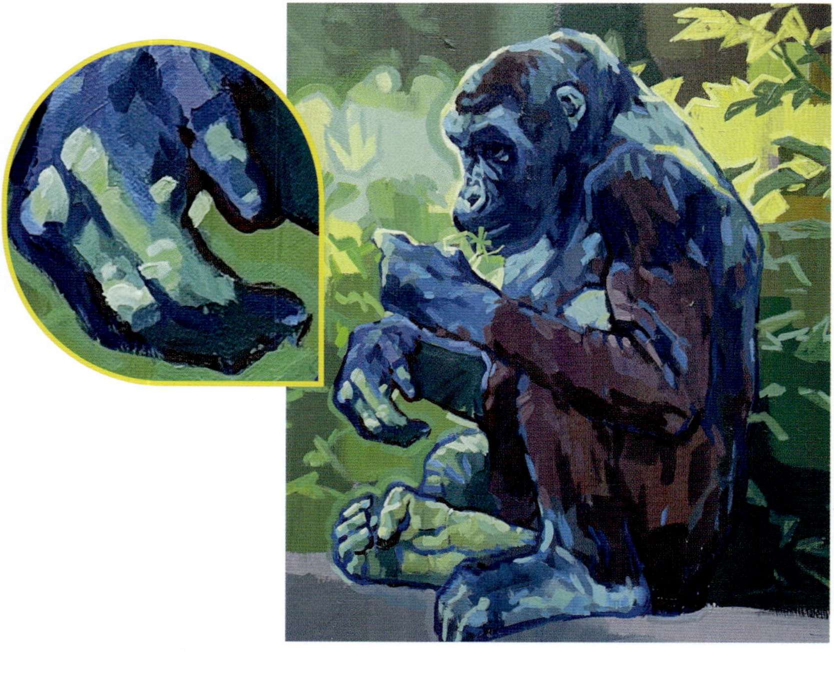

ADDING AN EDGE

Once the main elements of your painting are blocked in, pick a colour appropriate to your scene. Use a round brush to begin lassoing some shapes by outlining them. Use some broken lines to avoid a continuous edge, and vary the thickness as you apply them. You'll notice straight away the shapes become coherent and defined.

Don't overdo it as this would make everything stand out – and thus emphasize nothing. Try using different colour lines to create interest; the last few lines can be delicate and applied with a finer brush. Think about the quality of your line by varying pressure or by using a larger brush for linework.

Compare these two images to see how adding outlines has allowed me to add detail and draw the eye to areas of interest.

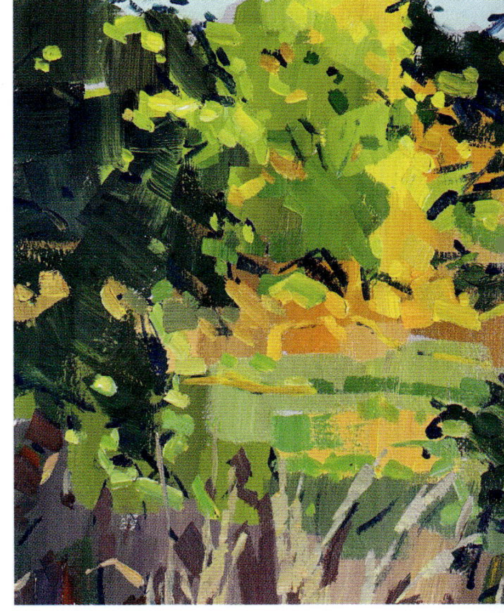

ABOVE RIGHT:

At this early stage, the shapes are blocked in, and there are various soft or underworked edges. The eye drifts through the painting.

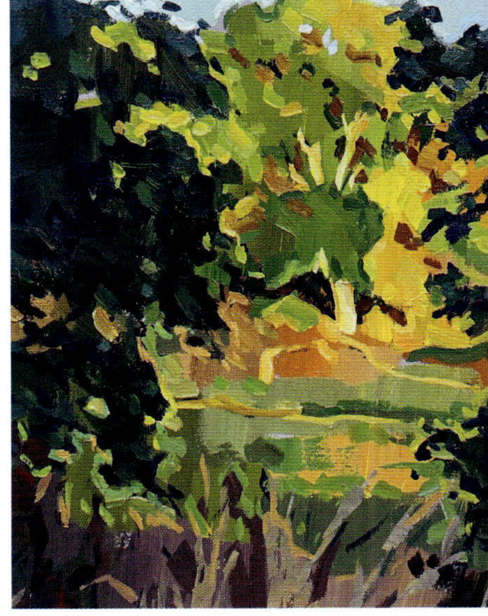

RIGHT:

Some of the foreground grasses have been outlined to give a more definite presence; and the central tree is now easier to read. More subtly-toned outlining is visible in the darker foliage too, helping to resolve the shapes.

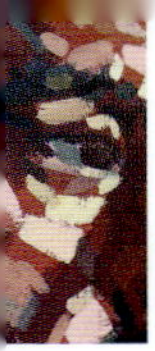

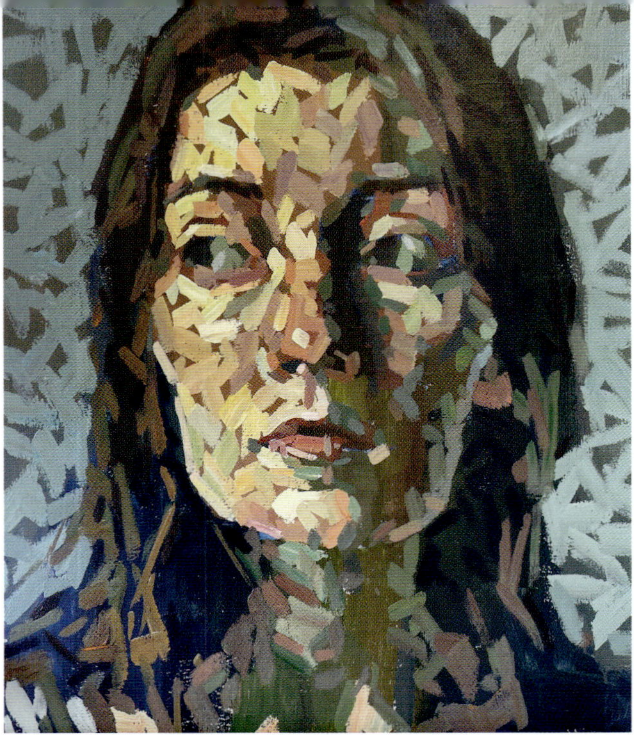

One-hit wonder

You can say something impactful by building up a series of small brushstrokes – the result is a little like a mosaic, but with dabs of colours rather than tiles. This exercise is helpful if you overwork your paintings.

Place each brushstroke side by side – some can overlap a little, but try to avoid blending or layering too much. In the portrait example above and opposite, you can see how the blocks condense to give you a strong overall image.

Be brave

The marks you make should vary subtly in colour and scale, but always be bold and strong. It's vital to avoid revisiting the mark or you will lose the spontaneous nature of the technique.

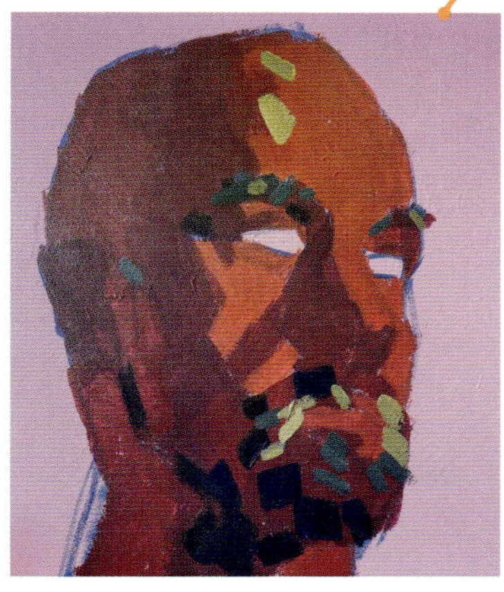

STAGE 1 Model the face with a base colour mix of diluted magenta and white.

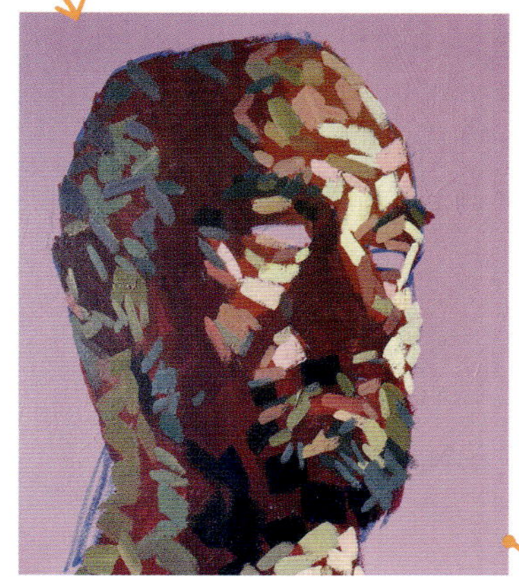

STAGE 2 Fill the face with blocks of varied colour, creating confident-looking marks.

Start by sketching with a range of flat tonal variations to model the face. Use your choice of colour here, as these marks will be mostly covered with the blocks of paint later.

Using neat acrylic, add light variations to immediately highlight the face. Start with soft reds which slowly meld into earthier browns, and leave some larger gaps to allow the marks to 'breathe'. Introduce contrasting cooler blocks of blues and greens mixed with the earlier colours.

Add contrasting darks and lights for facial hair, shadows and background. To finish, add the eyes with as few marks as possible, then stop: nothing should be over-painted.

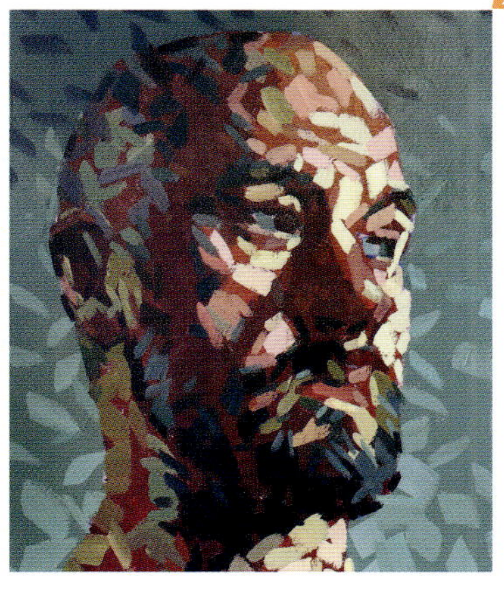

FINISHED PORTRAIT

A flat grey mix of of blues, reddish-browns and white was used for the background colour, with variations used to speckle the area.

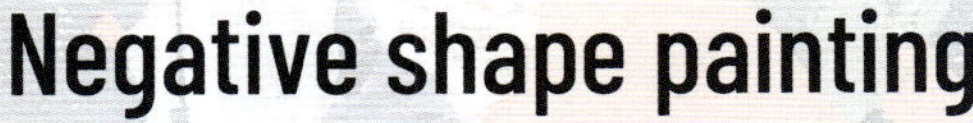

Negative shape painting

Positive shapes are the objects themselves – the bird and its perch in this example. **Negative shapes** are the shapes formed by the gaps between positive shapes.

Paint a parrot #2

Negative shape painting uses the background to throw the the positive shapes forward. This approach helps you to avoid becoming too conscious of painting the details of a parrot in the early stages, by placing it quickly, then refining the surrounding spaces to draw the bird out.

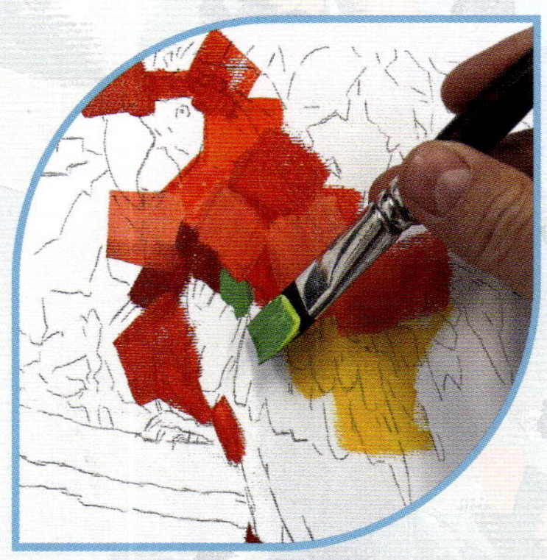

LOOSE BEGINNINGS Using a damp medium flat brush, apply blocky marks of a medium yellow to the back of the parrot, extending the paint past the drawn outline. Do the same with a variety of reds and orange, too. Work more carefully where colours meet.

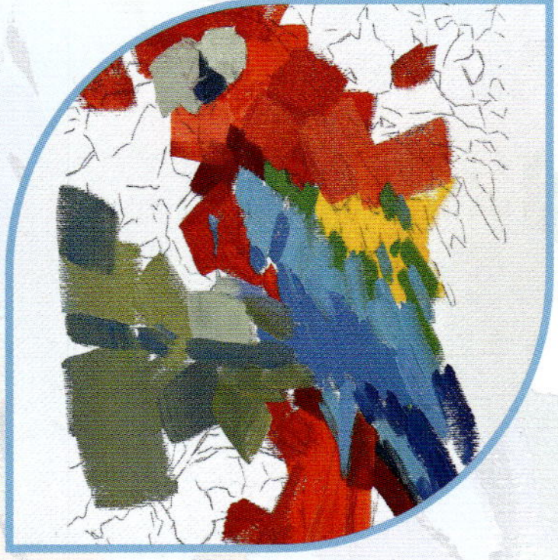

BUILD UP Working with semi-thick paint so you can still make out some of the drawn outline underneath, build up the parrot and its perch. These marks can break out of their outlines – we'll cut in to tidy up later. Allow these colours to dry before moving on to paint the negative shapes of the background.

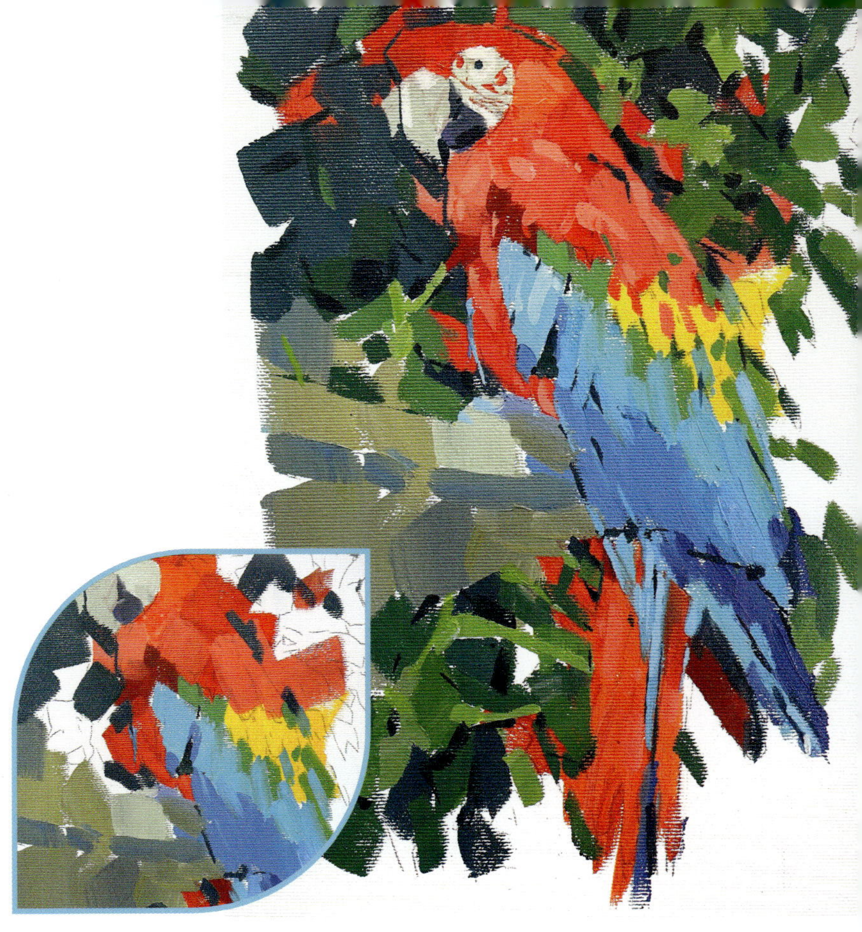

CUTTING OUT Using a dark tone mixed from sap green and violet, begin to carefully carve out the parrot, using the marks of the brush to overlap and reshape the parrot. Vary the mix with white to soften areas, and use a mid to light green mix of sap green, yellow, blue and white to fill in more background and paint around the parrot.

THE FINISHED PARROT

Allow some of the initial colours to filter through the background, as this will link the positive and negative spaces. Add any additional fine detail at the end.

Colour schemes

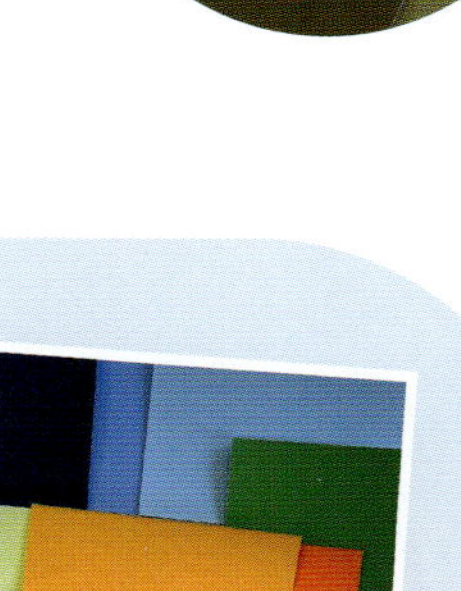

You can follow the colours in your reference material but rainy scenes don't have to be grey or landscapes overwhelmed with greens. Creating a colour scheme will help you make your scene balanced or dynamic, with a greater sense of design. Use small coloured cards to create swatches for ideas on colour schemes. Start with up to six colours to keep things mainly harmonious, with just one or two accented colours to create contrast – as in the examples to the right.

Colour cards are a great way to experiment before brush touches canvas. Here, a hot pink accent makes these muted schemes pop.

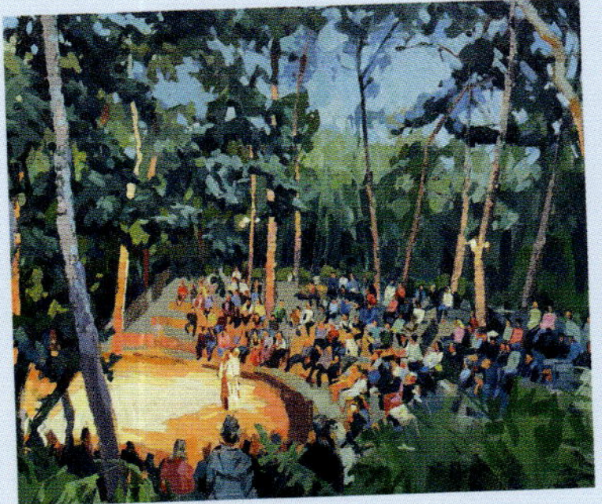

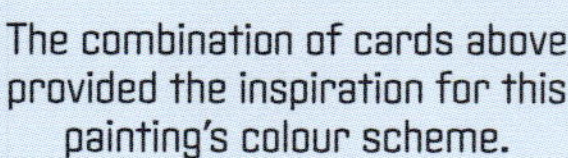

The combination of cards above provided the inspiration for this painting's colour scheme.

FROM REFERENCE TO SCHEME – IDEAS

- *Choose a scene to paint and try to replicate the scheme.*

- *Flip things on their head: create a striking colour scheme first and use it to paint your reference.*

- *Start from a black and white reference photograph, and create a colour scheme for it.*

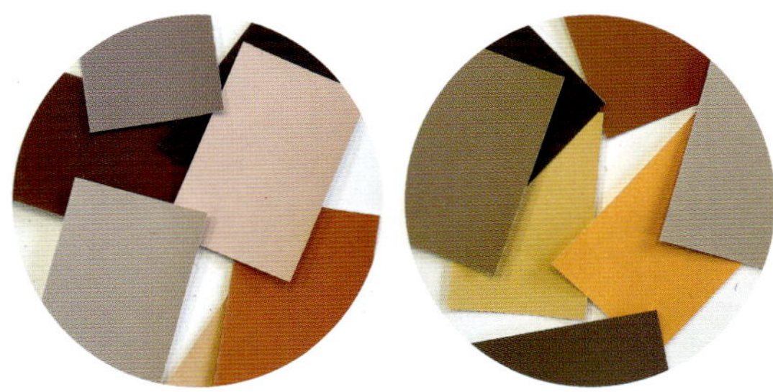

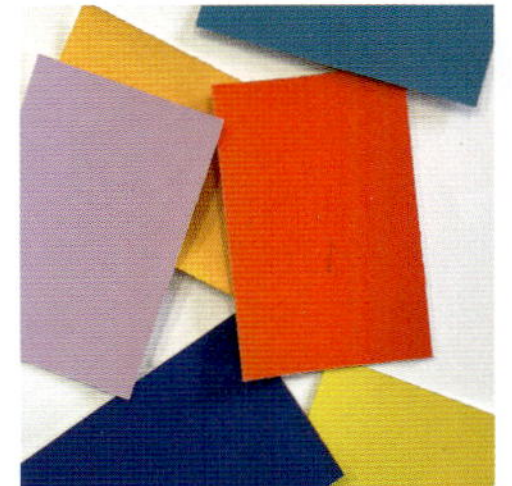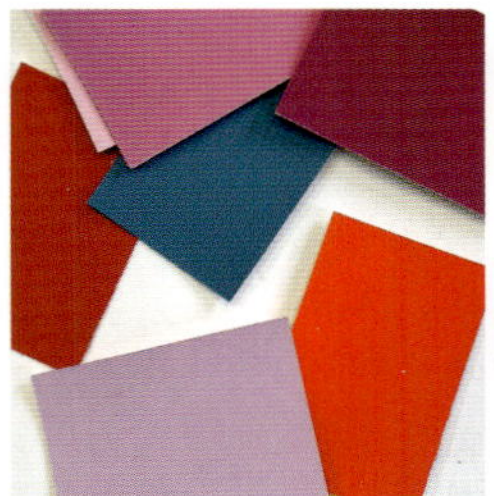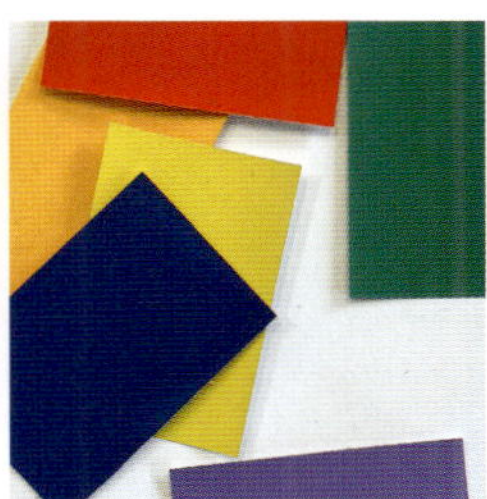

One step beyond

As you grow in experience, add more complicated, less
predictable combinations.

PHYSICAL CARDS

You can make your own colour cards by purchasing coloured sheets or
purchase packs of pre-cut coloured cards.

You can use various apps or books on colour but I like the immediacy of
grabbing a few colours, laying them out and seeing how they behave. You
can photograph various schemes for reference to be used later in a painting.
This additional planning makes life easier when producing artwork as you'll
know your colours and that they work.

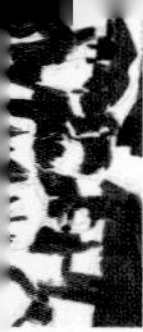

Notan

I've written before about the Japanese design concept of *Notan* – *'light and dark harmony'* or *'balance'* – and I really do love it's simplicity. In a nutshell, you render an image in stark black and white with no or very few mid-tones – this creates interesting compositions and helps to avoid stressing over detail.
This helps to identify and create a very clear direction of light, which is invaluable when composing a scene or breaking down a complicated one. It's a very easy way to showcase the passage of light while creating interesting shapes on the way.

Notan filters out unnecessary information leaving large shapes which in turn produce interesting outlines.

You'll discover all kinds of interesting shapes as you meld elements together.

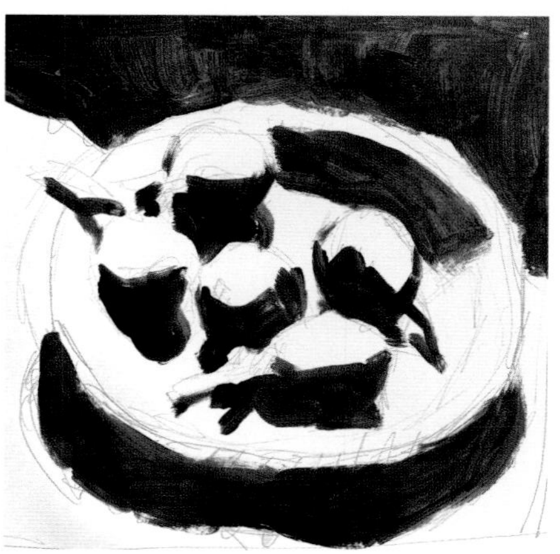

SIMPLE *NOTAN* BOWL OF FRUIT

*The arrangement of the fruit is immediate
when just black tone against white is used.*

The two main figures here contain elaborate, smaller diagonals where
the background shapes have been flattened. Things could be simplified
even more by blocking in more shapes with dark. When it comes to
painting the scene as a finished artwork, you'll know your focal points
and which areas to play down.

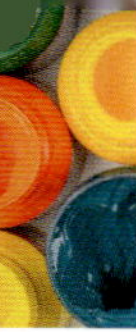

Colour mixing

If you have paints in the primary colours of red, yellow and blue, you should be able to mix plenty of other colours.

We all know that red and blue make purple, but there are many reds and many blues – we might call these different hues 'colour families'. Those you choose to mix will affect the resulting purple – giving you anything from a rich imperial purple to a muddy near-brown.

This is because within each family of colour there are subtle variations that will impact on the colour mixing.

LIMITED COLOUR PALETTES

Limiting your colours has a number of advantages. Having fewer colours makes it less likely to produce muddy mixes, and also helps you get to know individual hues and how they interact with others.

Start with a few paints, get to know them, and then expand your palette with one or two new ones. After you have become familiar with these, repeat the process, until you can mix every colour you want.

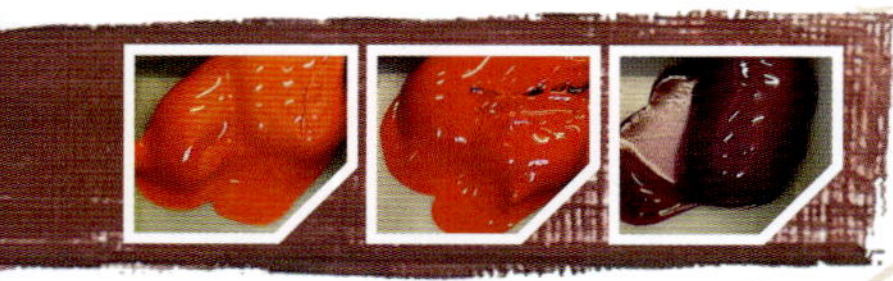

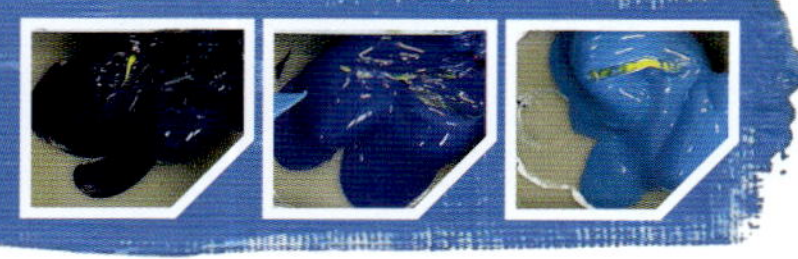

WARM AND COOL WITHIN FAMILIES

Here you can see warmer (on the left) and cooler (on the right) paints within two families of primary colours.

Mixes are cleaner when kept within a certain cool or warm range. As you begin mixing both cool and warm colours together you'll create more conflict in the range, so it's best to stick to either a cool or warm palette when mixing.

How many in the mix?

As a general rule, the more colours you mix, the harder it is to get clean, bright results.
The brightest, most vibrant colours will always be pure, unmixed paints.

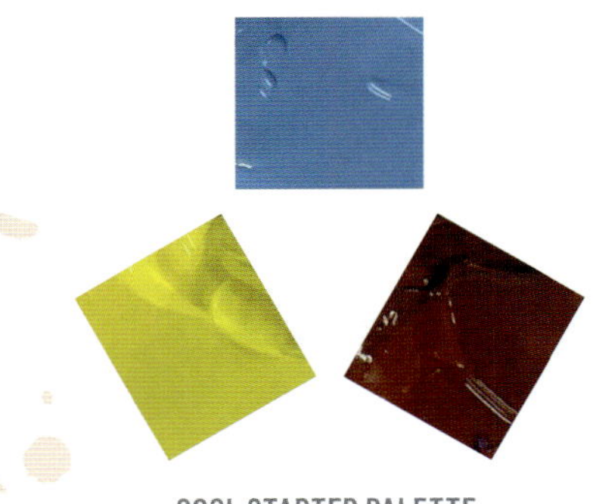

COOL STARTER PALETTE

Lemon yellow, phthalo blue and magenta red.

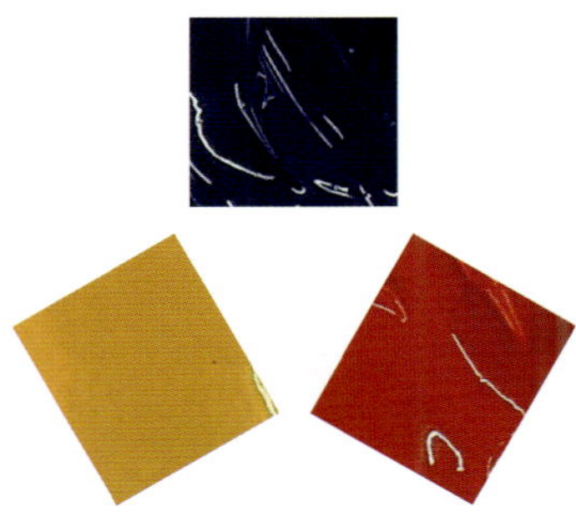

WARM STARTER PALETTE

Cadmium yellow medium, ultramarine blue and pyrrole red.

COLOUR TEMPERATURE

You may find it daunting choosing between families if you're new to colour theory. As a starting point begin to see colour as warm or cool versions.

Some pairs within families are only subtly different, while others are more obviously warmer or cooler.

Reds Vermilion red, for example, is very warm and yellow-tinged, while magenta red has clear blue leanings.

Yellows Lemon yellow is a cool yellow as it contains a hint of blue, while cadmium yellow medium is a warm yellow, as it contains traces of red.

Blues Cobalt blue is slightly warmer than the cool-tinged phthalo blue, and French ultramarine is warmer than both.

PIGMENT STRENGTH

Some pigments are inherently stronger than others. If you're looking for one colour to dominate a mix (say you want a green that leans more towards blue), remember that the quantities of each colour play a part. Experiment with different proportions to see if you can get the mix you want before adding another paint.

Mixing marvellous mud

Neutral earth tones are used in at least some way in most paintings. The mixes are made up of several colours so that no single hue dominates, and a muddy or earthy colour is born. However, there are good and bad muddy colours. You can buy tubes of ready-mixed brown paints such as raw umber or burnt umber which are convenient for explaining dark or neutral areas in paintings. Used on their own, however, these pigments can appear monotoned or repetitive.

THE CHALLENGE OF ACRYLICS

With acrylics, colours darken as they dry, and because they are opaque, they lack the 'glow' of watercolours or oils. This adds to the difficulty of mixing interesting earth tones.

USING COMPLEMENTARIES

Pair up An alternative to using premixed earth colours is to mix complementary pairs: two colours from opposite sides of the colour wheel (see left). Because they are as far removed from each other as possible in terms of hue, they neutralize each other.

Clean or dirty? Mixing two pigments will create a more interesting, clean neutral than using lots of colours: the more different paints you add, the more the impurities muddy the mix.

Gain control Using fewer colours also gives you control. It's then easier to allow one colour to dominate a little. Red and green, for example, create a lovely brown – and simply adding a little more of one or other of these colours will provide a bias: a greenish-brown or reddish-brown. Subtle variations across an area of your painting will help you avoid a monotone look.

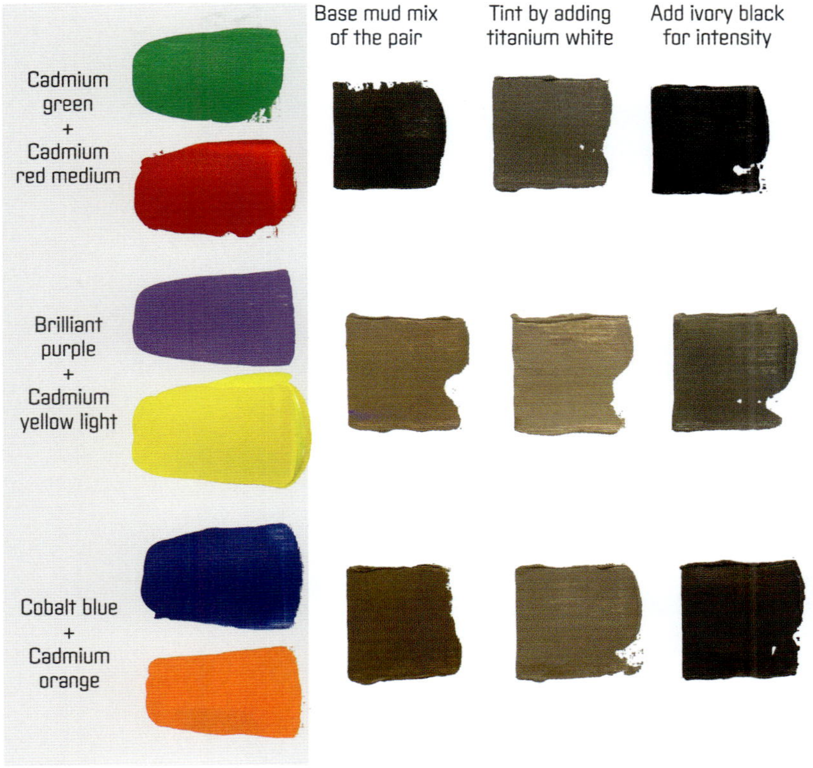

	Base mud mix of the pair	Tint by adding titanium white	Add ivory black for intensity
Cadmium green + Cadmium red medium			
Brilliant purple + Cadmium yellow light			
Cobalt blue + Cadmium orange			

COMPLEMENTARY PAIRS FOR SUCCESSFUL MUD

Shown here are some examples of the earth colours you can mix from the complementary pairs shown. From the base mud mix, you can add white to create lighter tints or add black for more intense tones.

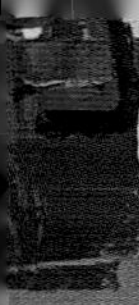

Dominant black

A common preconception for new artists is that they must avoid using black. It's true that it dominates and can dull colours when mixed – but its use can also give great impact.

- The advantage of using black in your artwork is its ability to calm ferocious colours.

- It's also great to practise at the boundaries of colour and tone – this builds confidence and makes for more striking artworks.

- Colour evokes the emotional response, while black frames and defines shapes. Combining the two elements makes for a potent combination.

Using black

Start by practising with some quick painted studies. Just play with colour and black or choose a simple subject such as an object, single flower or fruit. Try applying strong colour first, avoid too much mixing or over blending. Allow to dry and apply black around the scene to balance the colour. Get a feel for how much black is enough. Next, try mixing small amounts of black with colour estimating how much completely dulls the colour and how much creates interesting shades. Allow some of the colour to come through neat without black in the mix.

Different tools for different schools

Artists from the Impressionist school favoured rich colours and avoided black, while Expressionist artists used black freely in their artwork. Treat it like any other tool: to be used for a particular purpose.

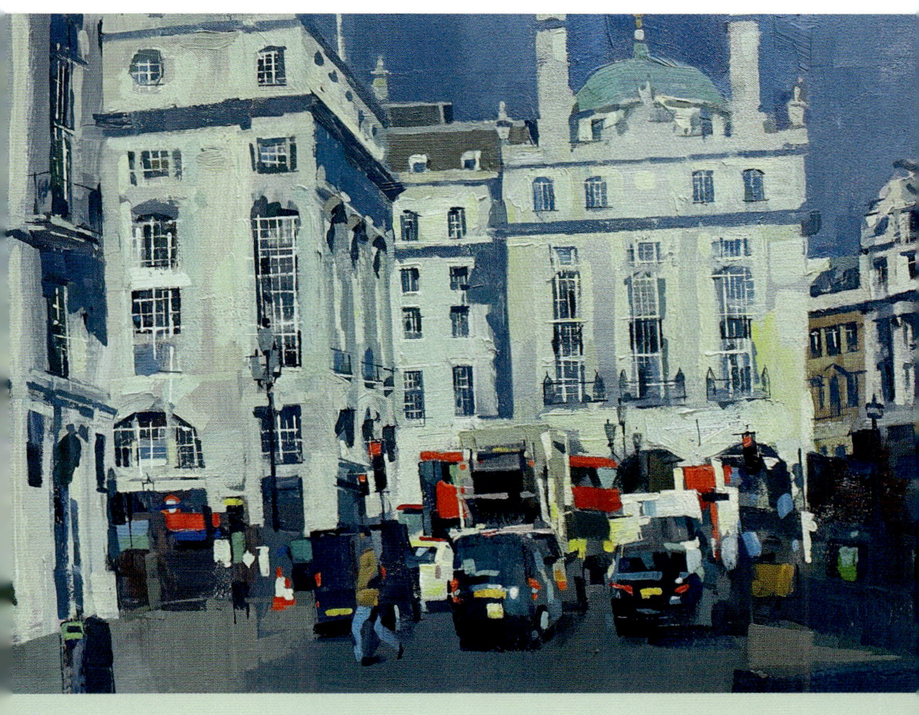

*Example of a street scene using black in shades
and rich colour nearby for optimum contrast.*

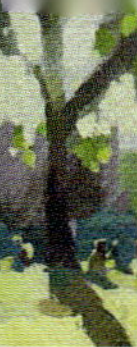

Break the harmony

Some scenes contain one main colour that dominates throughout. This can be an advantage as similar families of colours create a harmonious vibe – but with no colour contrast to help create impact, it can also look a little dull.

You can break the tendency of harmonious colours to look monotonous by introducing a complementary of the dominant colour. The key is to use a smaller percentage of a supporting colour against the main one to avoid colour conflicts.

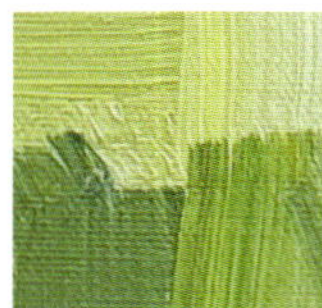

Dominant harmonious greens.

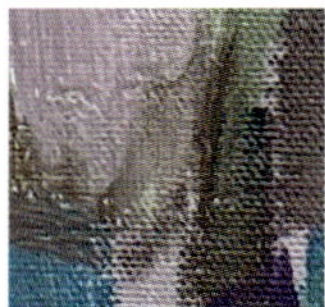

Complementary violets and browns.

PAINTING PARKLAND

Landscapes or park scenes provide lots of practice with greens. The complementary of green is red, so add small amounts of shades of red or reddish brown to contrast. You can also use violet to contrast the yellowish greens.

For the example shown, begin by using a flat brush to block in the main shapes using neat acrylic paint. Use a mix of greens with small dabs of Prussian blue and introduce white to the mix for light greens and yellow tints. For darker shades, use dark blue with greens with a tiny amount of black. Introduce light violet in the background, along with reddish brown in the trees and skin tones. The reddish brown is a mix of cadmium red and sap green.

Once dry, use a smaller brush to develop details – but avoid too much refinement. The early stages provide the colour scheme and overall balance – use the latter stages to optimize highlights (I use larger amounts of white with various yellows), while stronger darks are used sparingly in the foreground.

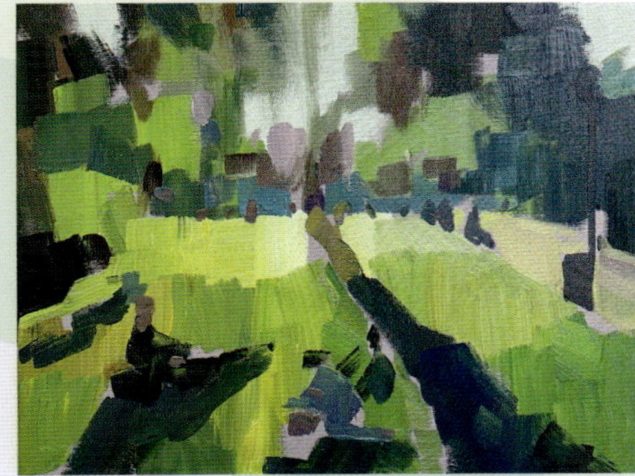

BLOCKED-IN COLOUR

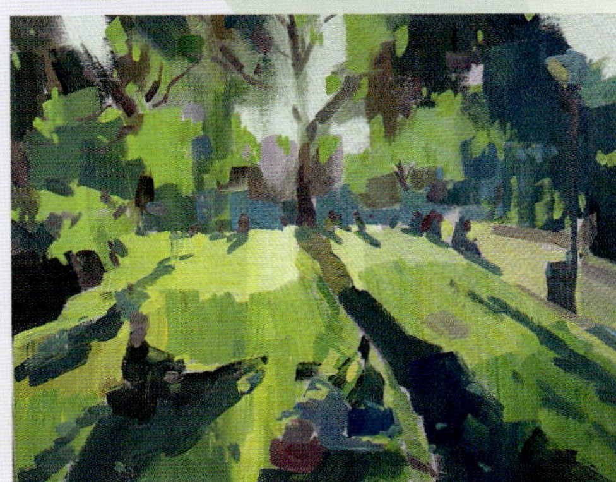

SMALLER BRUSH WORK

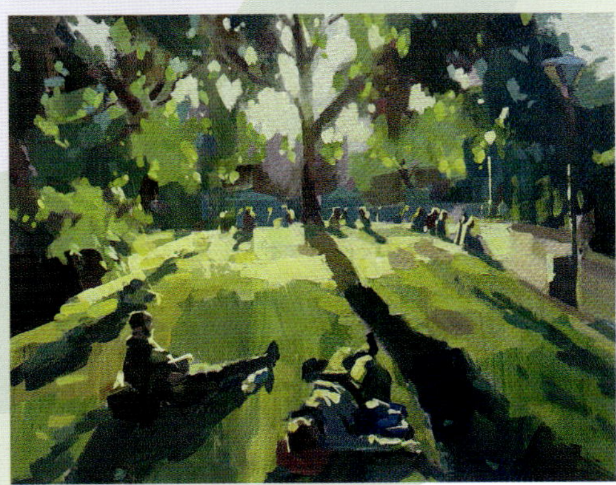

CONTRASTING LIGHT AND
DARKS, PLUS CRISP DETAIL

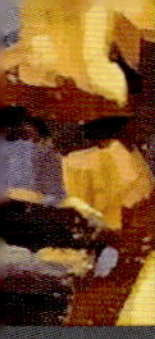

Base colour

If you paint on white paper or canvas, the white will illuminate the colours you applied – but flickers of white visible through the layers may diminish the strength of highlights you later apply.
Painting the surface with a flat **base colour** before you begin adds some tonal value, which allow highlights to pop. A mid- to light grey is traditional but a little dull, so try adding a touch of green, blue or red to perk it up. It's well worth experimenting to find interesting combinations.
Using a base colour is a great first step in considering a process and not simply painting a scene. This should be the start of looking at other additions you can add to your artwork for dramatic effect.

Choose a neutral base colour to keep the scene calm, and a bright colour to add vibrancy.
A base colour that contrasts with the main colours you will use will create eye-catching impact.

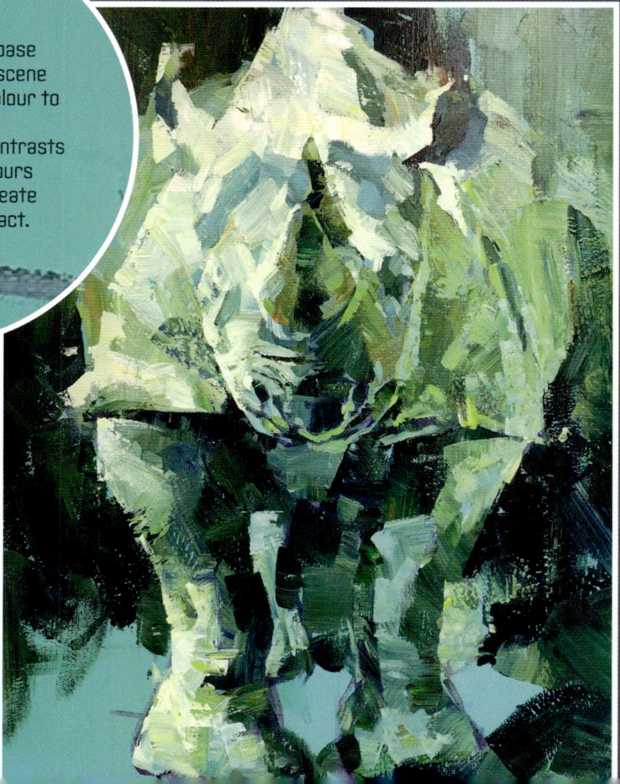

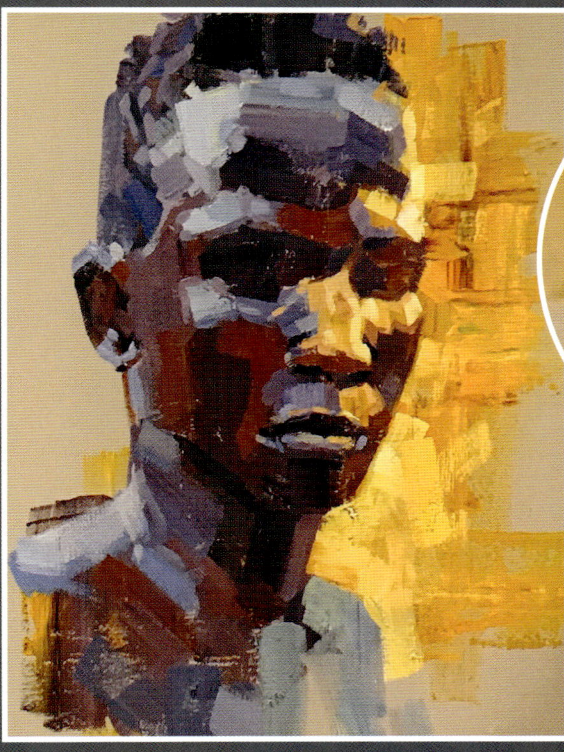

Turn up the base

- Base colours are a great way to unify a painting: simply leave flecks of the colour showing through at the end, as shown in the paintings here.

- Painting a green field on a magenta or purple base colour will create a dramatic contrast. The same is true for a green or turquoise base colour for a portrait.

- I prefer one strong base colour rather than lots of colours interweaving into one another, particularly for complex scenes, which can become too busy.

- Try a textured base colour by applying modelling/texture paste to your support before painting – or simply painting over an old unwanted painting.

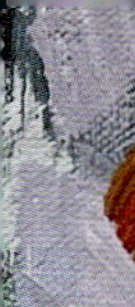

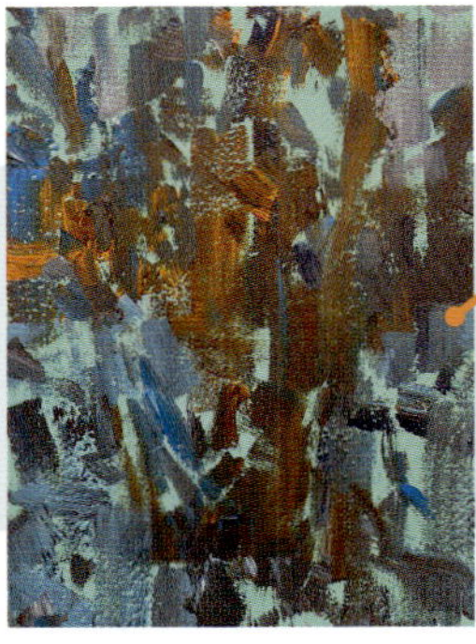

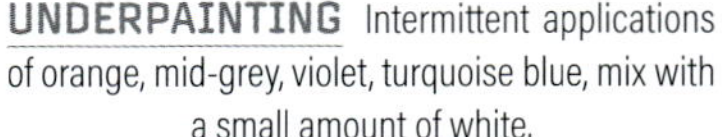

UNDERPAINTING Intermittent applications of orange, mid-grey, violet, turquoise blue, mix with a small amount of white.

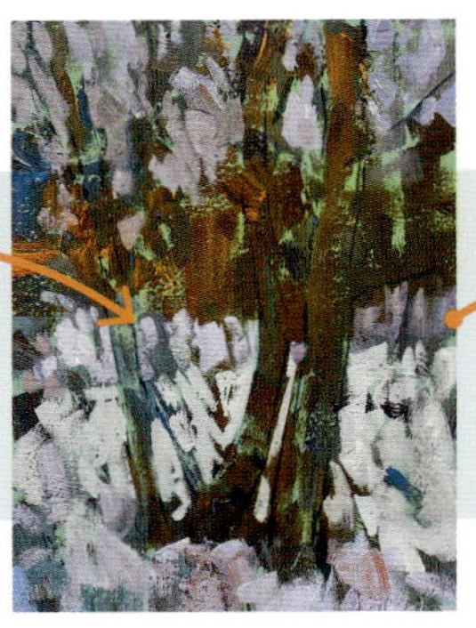

COOL LAYER Outline painted in dark blue; begin with light cool mixes, grey/blue and violet mixed with white.

Colourful snow

With grey skies and a generous coverage of snow, winter scenes can sometimes appear almost monotone. Finding colour in these scenes can be tricky, but it is there. Here are some tips for atmospheric snow scenes.

- Your starting point is colour temperature. Grey skies mean less warmth, so the majority of the painting will contain cool colours – look for blues, greens or purples.

- When creating your mixes, bear in mind that the overall light is subdued, so mix your colours with small amounts of grey or earthy shades to knock out some vibrancy.

- You'll need white to lighten colours which can make colours look chalky. Try dominating these mixes with a little more colour and less white.

- To set off areas of dull, neutral colour, add an accent of richer colour nearby.

- As you introduce contrasting warm colours into the painting, try mixing small amounts of the cools into the warms to connect and soften colour.

- Add texture and depth to snow scenes by beginning the painting with random marks using a few mid-tone colours, not too dark or nothing with too much white.

- Avoid covering entire areas; instead leave some base colour or white canvas showing through.

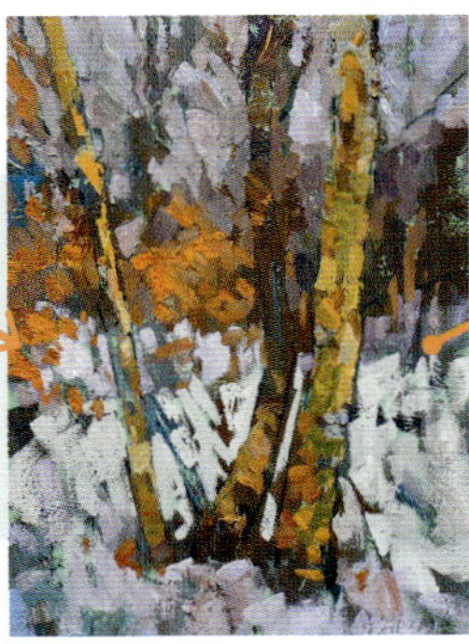

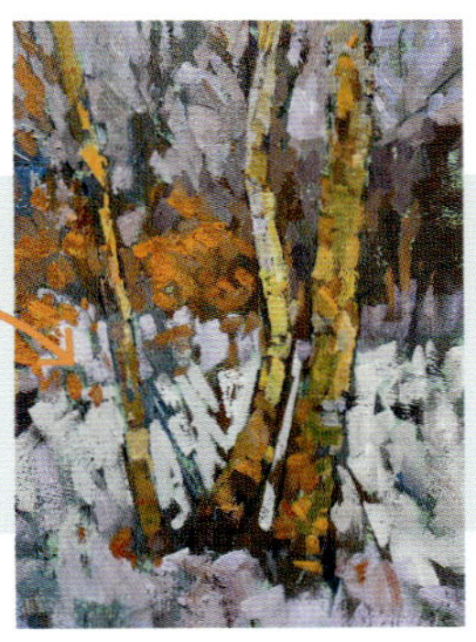

WARMING Introduction of warmer colours varying between orange, sienna and ochre. Enhance the shapes and introduce cool tints into warm colours.

DETAILS Finalize details with dark tones and fill in more base colour in the background.

Warm orange leaves create an accent to the blue-grey sky and snow.

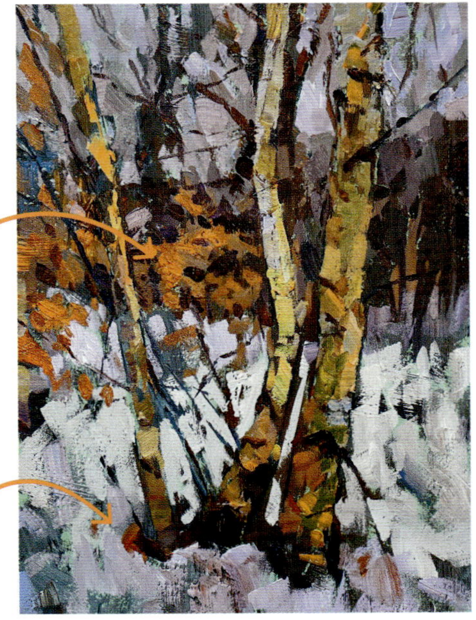

Use varying pressures when adding your mid-tone colours so there are thick and thin applications. This will create an interesting base to work on.

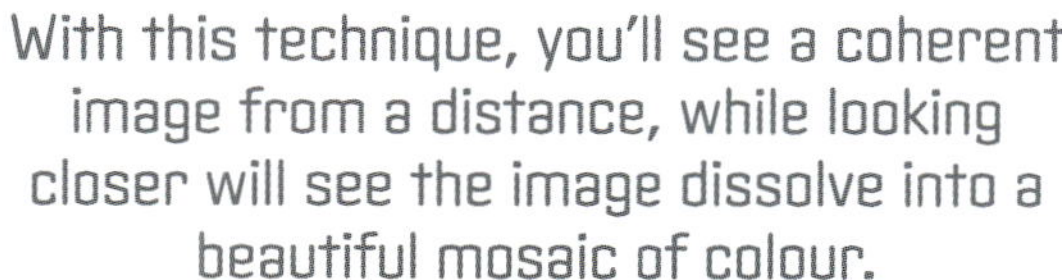

With this technique, you'll see a coherent image from a distance, while looking closer will see the image dissolve into a beautiful mosaic of colour.

Optical colour mixing

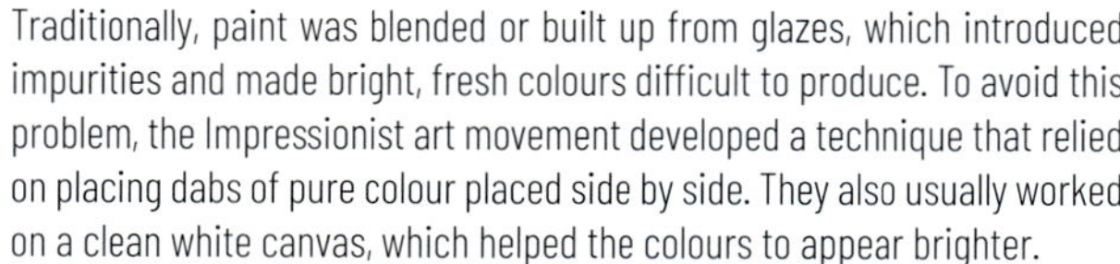

Traditionally, paint was blended or built up from glazes, which introduced impurities and made bright, fresh colours difficult to produce. To avoid this problem, the Impressionist art movement developed a technique that relied on placing dabs of pure colour placed side by side. They also usually worked on a clean white canvas, which helped the colours to appear brighter.

When viewed from a distance, the colours appear to interact, and give a brighter, fresher feel than using paints physically mixed together. The technique is called 'optical colour mixing'. It can be time-consuming, as every mark is considered.

Paint a parrot #3

This technique helps in understanding colour theory and mark-making possibilities when incorporating brushmarks of different sizes and directions alongside varied pigments. If it's your first time using this technique, just keep everything simple with consistently-sized brush marks.

Draw your parrot onto clean white acrylic paper, with no base colour. Start with the red of the parrot, applying small distinct marks across the area, and mixing in orange, light violet, yellow, black or white to vary the hue. This process is particularly suited to acrylics as there's no traditional blending, pigment is applied and the blends appear by placing a dark or light version next to it.

Once the reds are in place, move on to the other colours in the parrot in turn, then on to the dark and light greens of the leaves

Finish off with smaller refining blocks to draw detail forward.

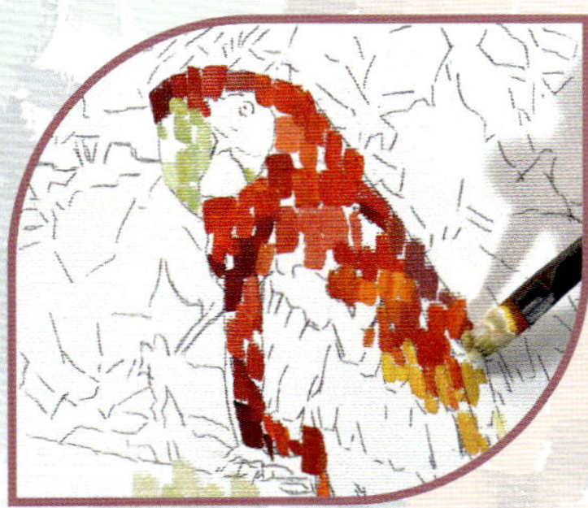

VARY THE HUE Use a small flat brush to apply varied dabs of colour. Avoid using the same hue too regularly by adding dabs of other colours, or varying the tone.

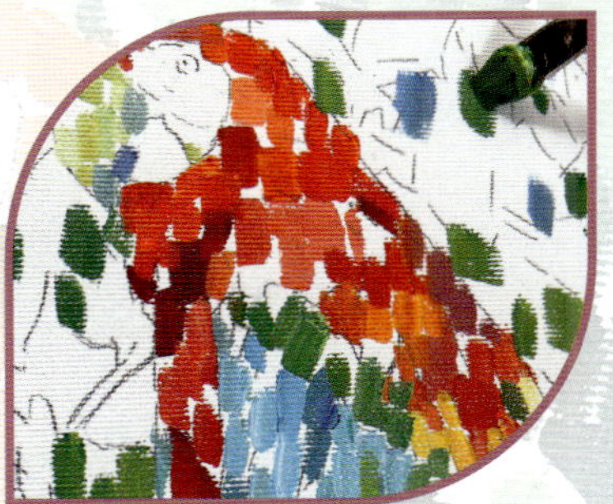

LINK THE BACKGROUND As you work, apply small marks to the background occasionally, using colours from the parrot. This will help to bind the picture together.

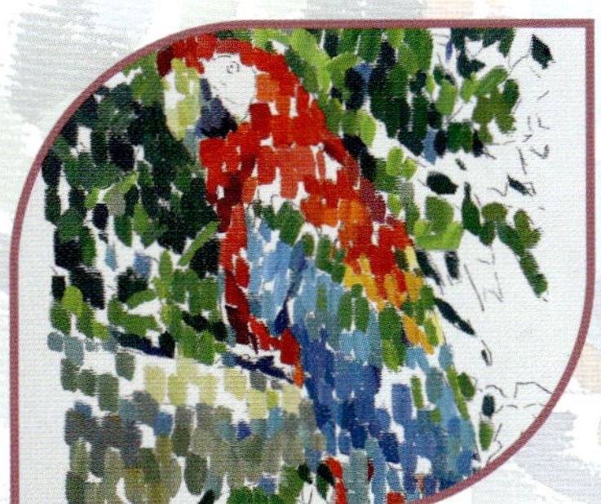

LEAVE GAPS As you work, avoid finishing areas completely. Leaving some small gaps will provide opportunities to add any additional colours you introduce.

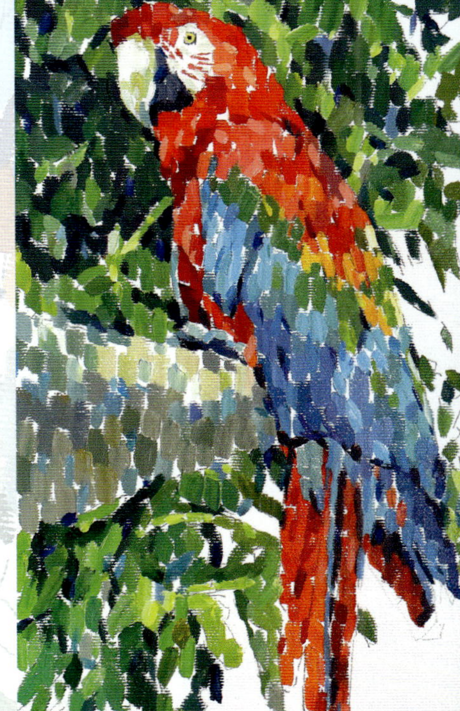

THE FINISHED PARROT

The final refining marks should cover some of the gaps, but leave some – even at the end.

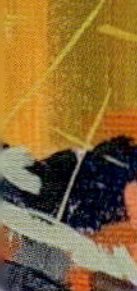

Work quicker, work brighter

Working quickly encourages more direct use of the paint, so colours look cleaner and brighter. As there's no time to consider mistakes, your process will become more intuitive and instinctual.

This is the exercise that changed my painting process for the better: from tight and representational to loose and impressionistic. I had lots of technical knowledge but not the intuitive painting instincts, so I set myself deadlines, even for simple exercises.

Spending no more than 45 minutes on each painting, I would stop on the dot, no matter what state the artwork was in. I continued this process until I could finish, feeling that no more was needed, before the time ran out.

Establish discipline through this exercise, and the technique will remain with you and all your future painting will be fresher, whether you work with a 45-minute deadline, a longer deadline, or no deadline at all.

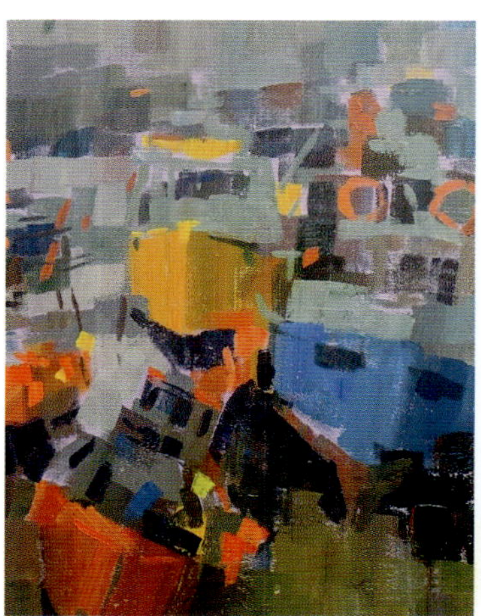

45 MINUTES FOR BASICS

This painting of boats measures 61 x 76cm (24 x 30in). 45 minutes in and the overall look is in place along with some tonal and colour contrasts – very little linework is done here.

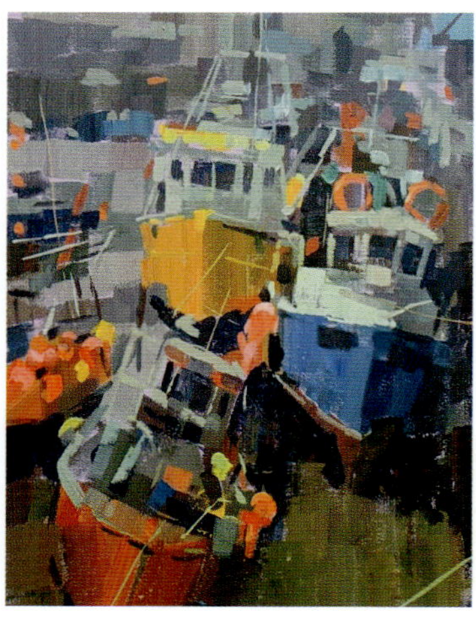

REFINEMENT: 45 MINUTES MORE

After another 45 minutes, richer highlights, tone, colours and precise detail are in. Much of the original mark making is still visible, with only certain areas enhanced.

PRACTICALITIES

Using large brushes benefits the process as areas are covered rapidly.

Even with a tight deadline, it's worth breaking the time limit down into various stages:

STAGE 1 Begin by loosely covering large areas so everything is addressed, creating a consistent look.

STAGE 2 Define shapes broadly so important elements start emerging.

STAGE 3 The last stage can be problematic as precise detail is applied which can soak up time. Ensure you do not lose track of time, and stop on the dot – or before!

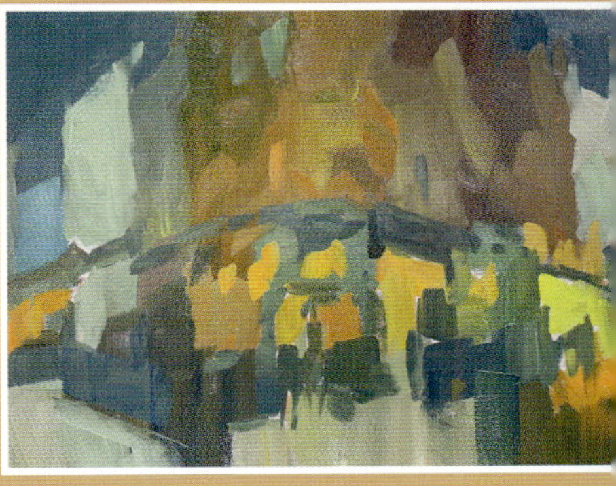

A complex street scene can be tackled through simplifying it at the first stage, as shown above.

Below you can see the finished version. which emphasizes colour, light and detail while retaining plenty of early applications.

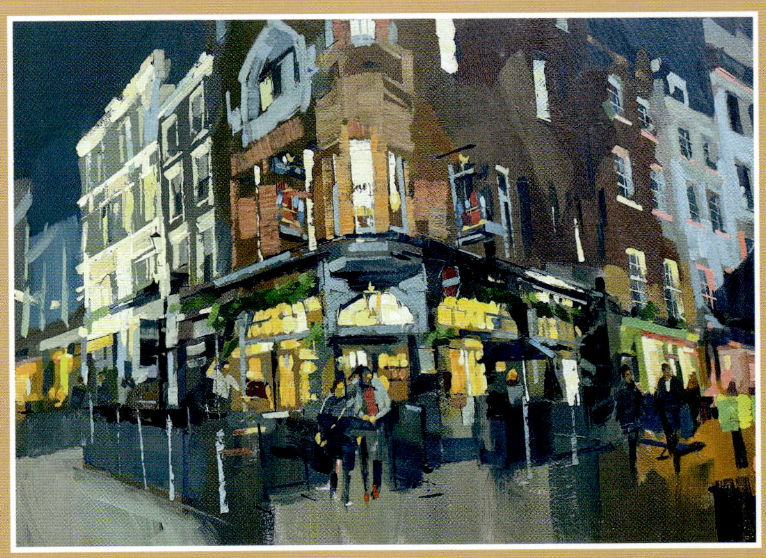

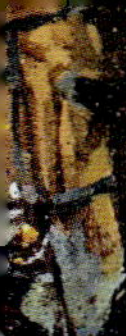

Edit your shots

Looking beyond your reference material is vital. It will help you to develop your own worldview for the scenes you paint, and help create a clear narrative. Simplifying the image can make what remains more engaging and ensures the finished painting makes a definitive point.

It can be quite tricky to decide how to edit a scene – sometimes you might add elements while others need removing. This example shows you what I've done to move from a promising but raw photograph to a finished piece with a clear narrative.

PUTTING IT INTO PRACTICE

I'll often look and revisit photographs I have taken to see how I can reinterpret the scene. Shown here is an example of a painting where the source material – see below – was severely edited to provide a clearer narrative of a horse and its rider. For this painting, I used acrylic spray paint with traditional heavy body acrylics.

Try the same yourself: find an image you like and consider which elements have the greatest effect on you. This could be something less obvious, such as colours, shapes or pattern – not simply the literal forms.

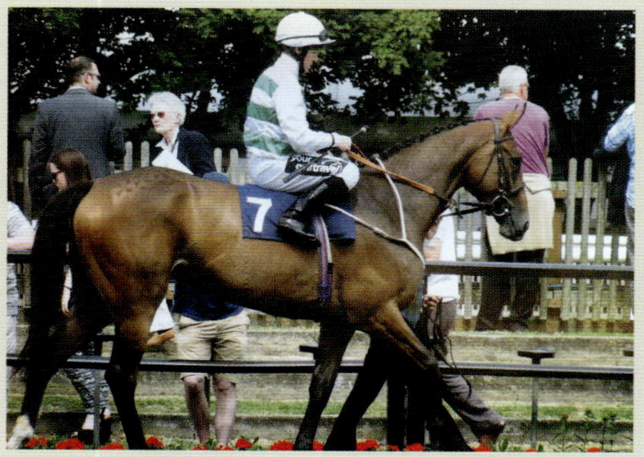

CUT THE CLUTTER

The original scene includes a jockey, horse, railings and figures in the background, along with overhanging trees.

I loved the jockey and horse, but everything else clutters the scene and distracts from my main interest.

A dark background, clear of additional elements, draws the lights forward and creates a neutral tone so the subject stands out.

The jockey's face is just hinted at, so that attention isn't distracted from the main focus: the horse.

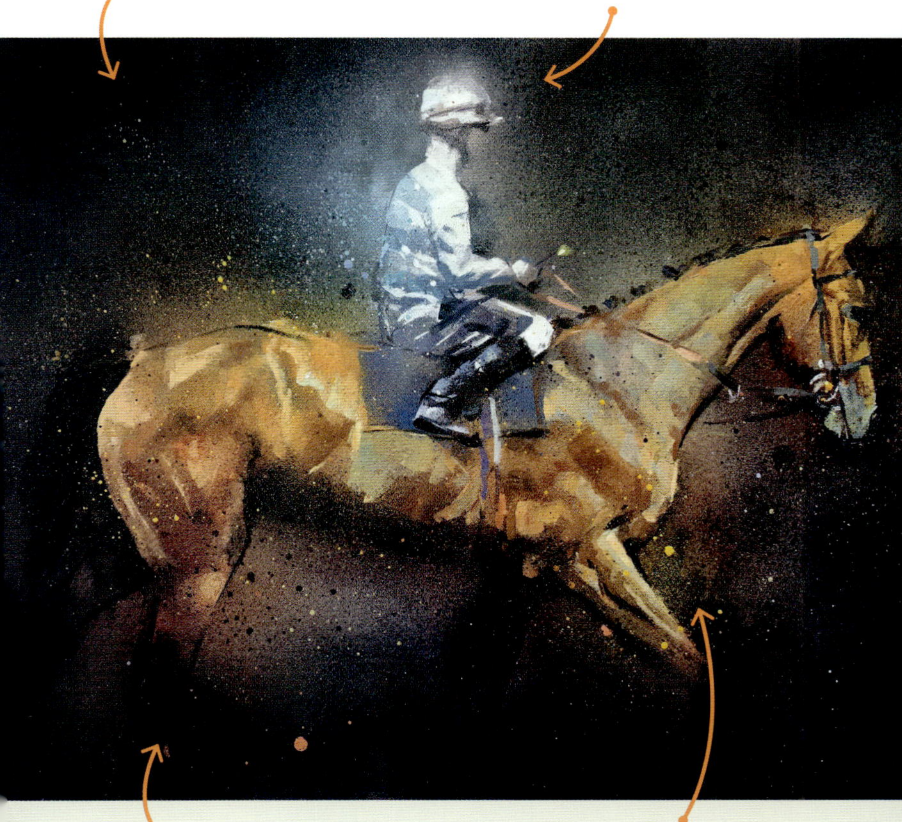

To avoid a cutout effect, the dark legs and shadows blur into the background.

The use of the spray paint (see page 30) creates lovely undertones of glowing colour. Larger speckles break edges and create interesting elements in themselves.

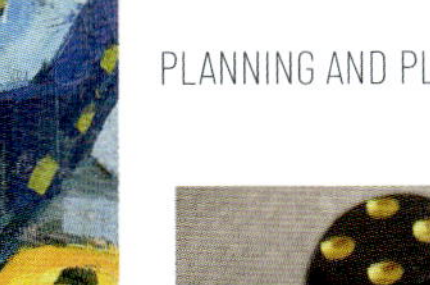

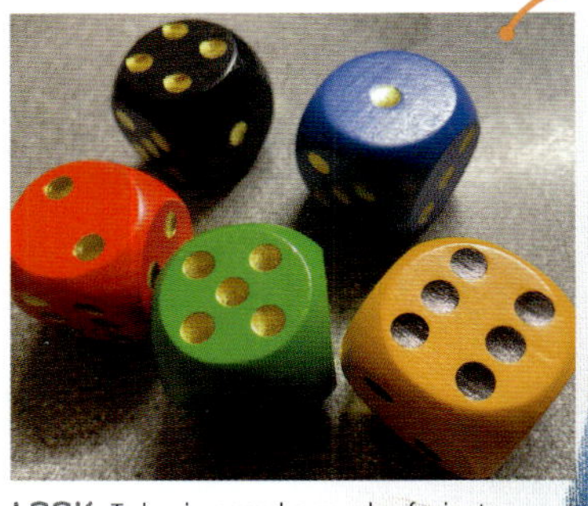

LOOK To begin, spend a couple of minutes looking at your reference image. Don't start any painting – just look at the image and soak up the information.

Chaos into order

For this exercise, choose an image with some strong accented colour – like these dice. You'll need it to be simple and memorable, as you'll spend the early part of the painting process not looking at your reference material. Before you start painting, make sure all your paints are ready and your canvas or paper is prepped.

CHAOS! Cover the photograph and for the next ten minutes use your memory to plot the course of the painting. You won't remember exact details or positions, so paint what you can remember: shapes or colour, direction of light and shadows and so forth. You'll end up with an almost abstract image. Once ten minutes are up, turn over the photograph and compare it with your work. You might be surprised at the accuracy (or lack thereof!) but either way, just embrace the chaos.

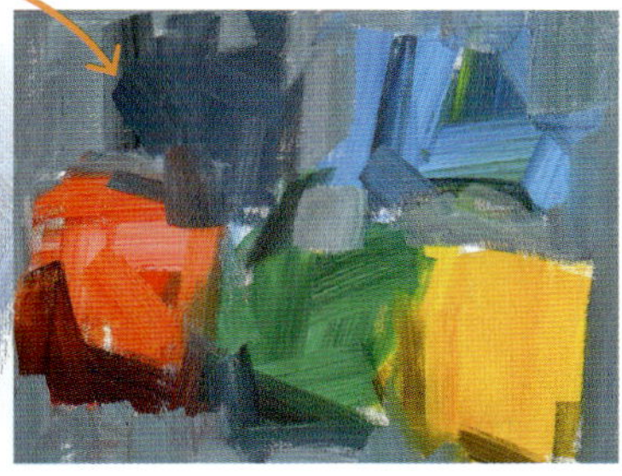

COLOUR AND DEPTH Begin shaping the objects by adding a background. Now you can see the reference image, start adding dark tones to begin drawing shapes forward. Avoid drawing everything and overwhelming the scene with too many darks.

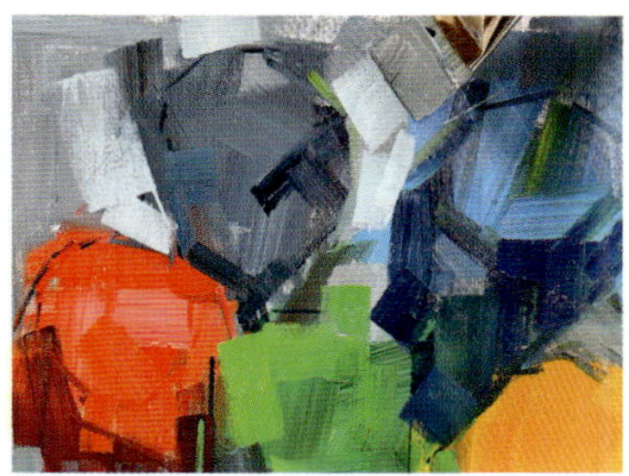

SHAPING AND LIGHT Having charted a course in defining shapes with darks, switch to using lights and tints to create contrast. Mix your tints by adding white to the colours used at the earlier chaotic stage.

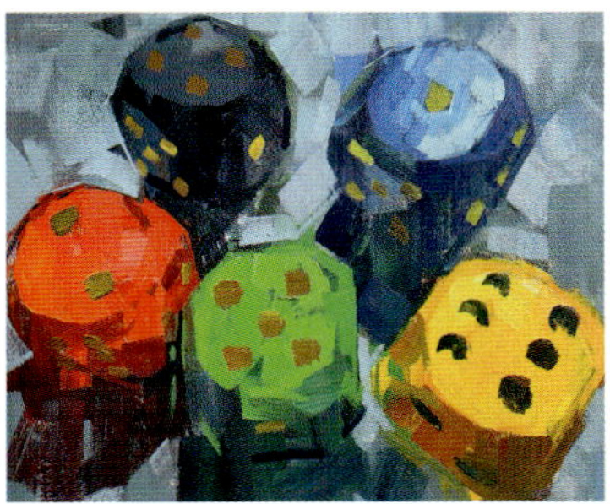

REFINE... As you work, you'll begin to see interesting pushes and pulls of highly defined edges against looser ones. Here, lighter and richer colours have been applied to the dice and details like the numbers were added.

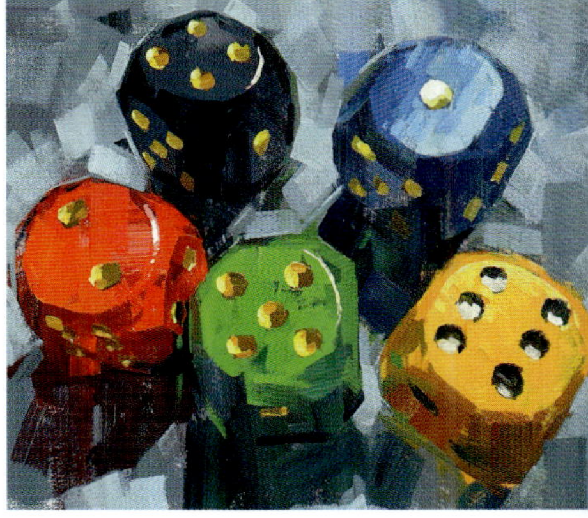

...BUT NOT TOO MUCH To ensure your finished painting retains some of the energy of the early chaos, stop while there is still an interesting balance between the uncontrived chaotic beginnings and the more considered, ordered marks that anchor the scene in reality.

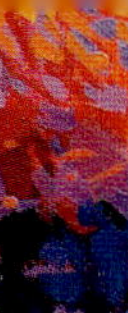

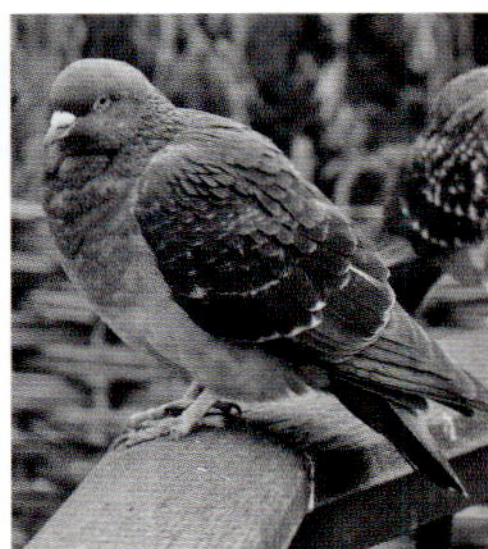

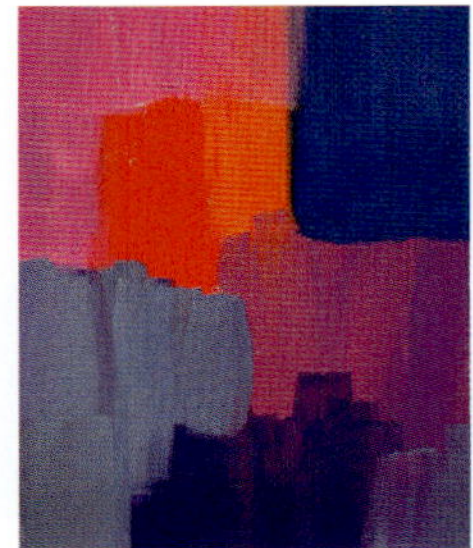

STAGE 1 Block in strong areas of colour to represent the warmest and coolest areas.

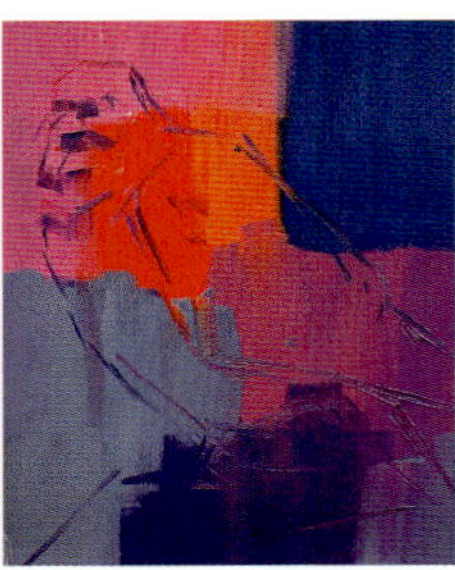

STAGE 2 Once dry, sketch in the pigeon with a neutral colour.

Black and white into colour

Working from a black and white reference photograph and picking your own colours will help build confidence in colour mixing.

Start by choosing cool and warm colours (see page 60) to use for the black and white tones in the photograph. This way you can assign colours knowing there's underlying logic. The light-toned areas in your photograph are lit by the sun, so treat them as warm, while the areas in shadow are cool. Mid-tone grey areas are somewhere in between, and here we can mix both warm and cool colours together.

Warms Pick yellows, reds or oranges for your warm areas.

Cools Choose blues, greens or violets for the cool areas.

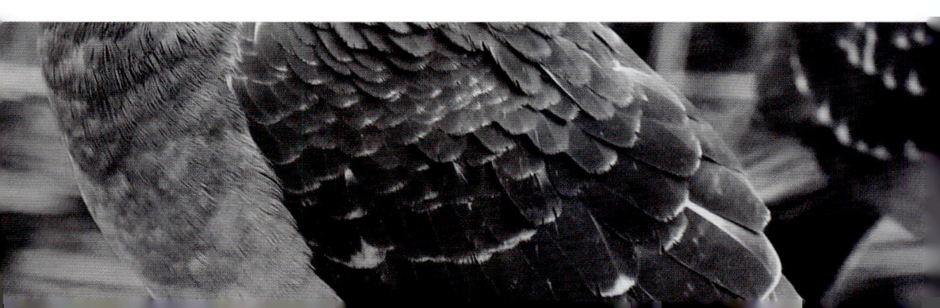

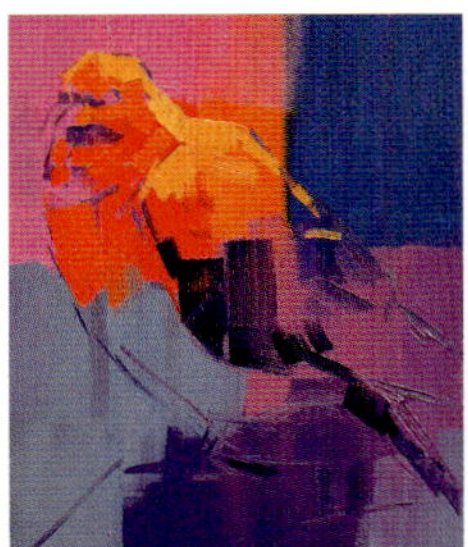

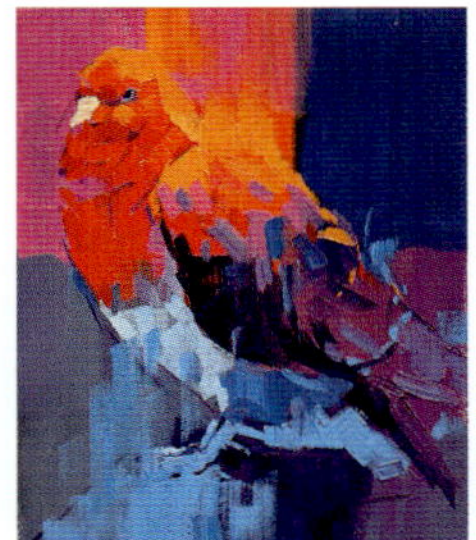

STAGE 3 Using variations of the underlying colour, add warms (reds and oranges) in the light areas, and deep violet in very dark areas.

STAGE 4 Use light blue on the lower half in shadow; mix red and blue to produce a magenta. for where warm and cool meet.

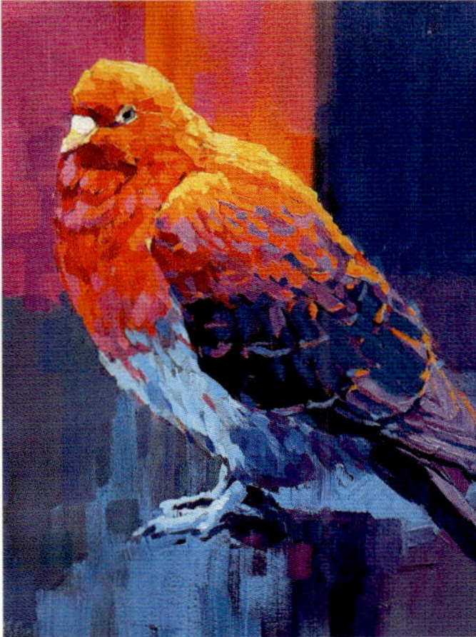

STAGE 5 Swap to a smaller flat brush for refinement, and include your richest lights and darks at this stage.

Follow this process to translate a black and white photograph of a pigeon into colour:

- Work on white canvas for bright results.
- I wanted to use red and pink for my warm colours, which led to my cool colour choices: blue is a complementary and violet contains both red and blue. Grey is included to neutralize the vibrant colour.
- Use a flat brush and semi-thick paint for the initial colours in stage 1.
- With the sketch in place, build up the pigeon with lighter and darker versions of the underlying colours.
- Mix more white and black into colours for optimum contrast.

Another idea

Instead of sticking with warms and cools, you can, of course, simply make up the colours you use – this is another great way to enjoy exploring colour.

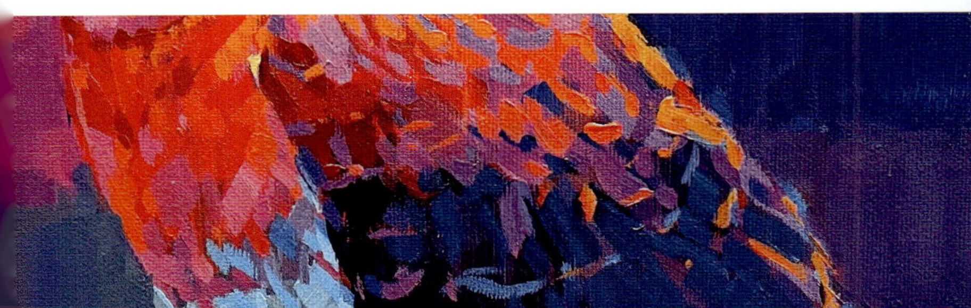

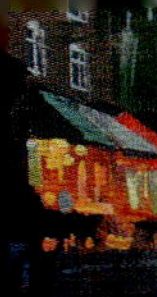

Flat areas

There are naturally occurring calm areas in scenes, such as big skies or foregrounds of rolling fields in a landscape. Depending on how complicated the scenes are, you might edit out or blur the information.

Flat areas in paintings are vital to create breathable, calm spaces against detailed ones. These flat areas provide the eye a chance to relax as looking at a cluttered scene creates confusion. This could be caused by the use of lots of clashing colours, excessive drawn detail or simply too many elements.

When starting out, there's an understandable tendency to try to include everything you see in front of you – but experience (and practice) will teach you the benefits of using empty space in a simple way.

Frame the focus

The street scene opposite shows how understated both the sky and foreground are to allow clearer focus for the main elements.

- Even though these areas are understated try to mix interesting combinations to create intriguing shades.

- Try using relatively thick paint with a large flat moist brush to create a weighty application – this adds a touch more depth to the layer.

- You can try adding variations of colour, but in general, simplicity is best: save up your concentration for the focal points.

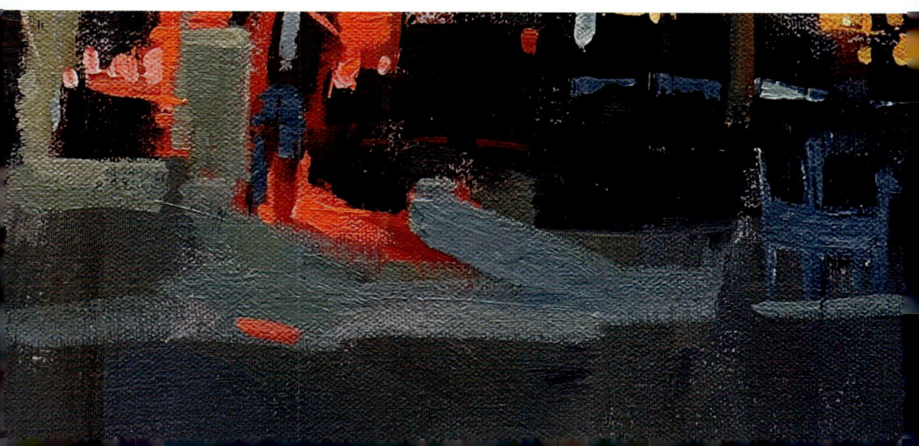

I've use a neutral colour for the sky, not quite light grey but an interesting mix of plenty of white with dabs of Prussian blue, red oxide, mid-yellow and sap green.

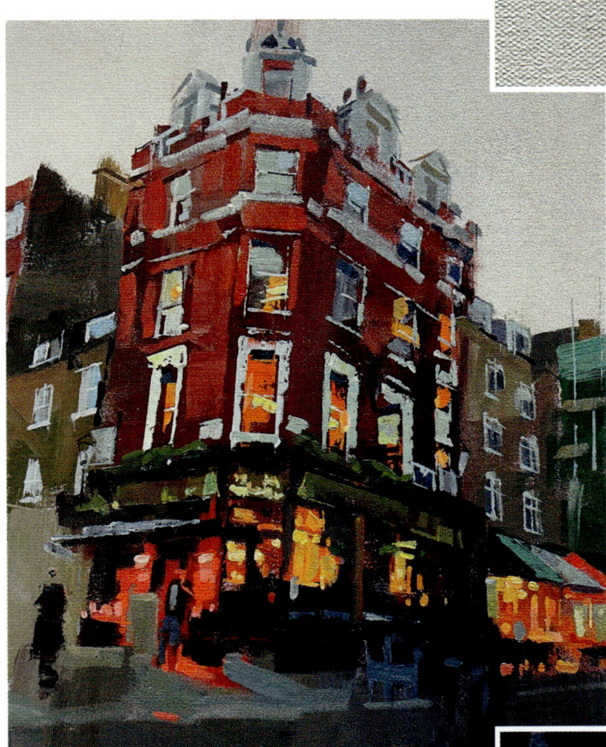

NEUTRALS AND DARKS

As a contrast to the flat light areas of the sky are the flat dark, neutral foreground areas. Again, these are made up of several colours: red oxide, sap green, black and Prussian blue with small amounts of white. The most intense darks are used to define the base of the building.

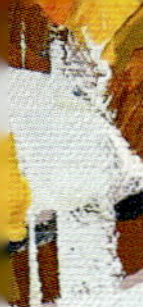

Glitching out

Losing lines, blurring edges and generally avoiding dictating everything will go some way towards engaging the viewer, by inviting them to interpret the blanks and add to the broken lines. There are plenty of ways to approach this but one way is to add 'glitchy' marks once you've completed a painting. In essence you're sabotaging the image and spoiling the painting. This adds to the intrigue of the artwork.

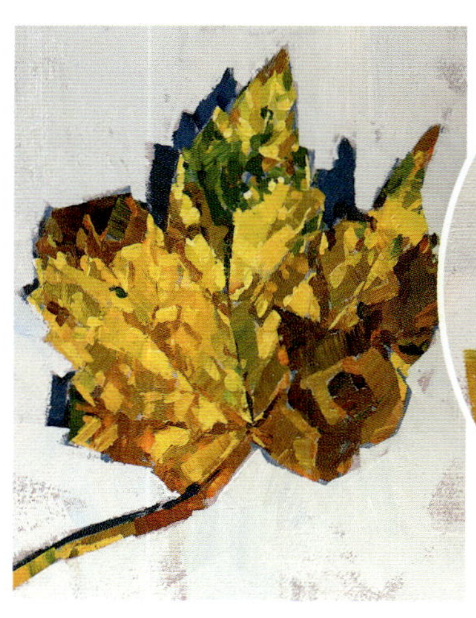

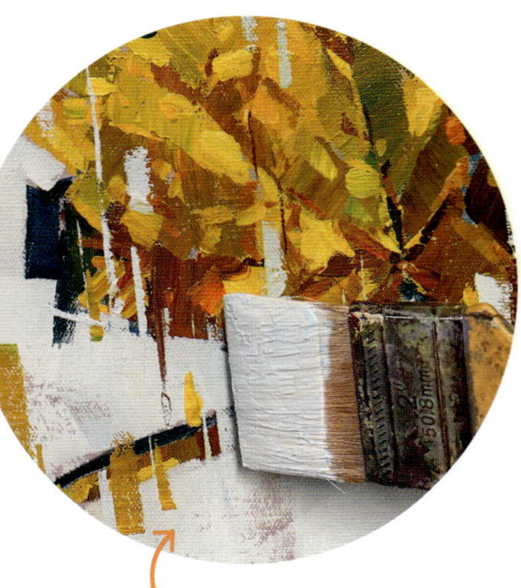

PAINTING

For this exercise, paint a simple subject, like this leaf. A limited palette makes this easier. Once your semi-realist subject is dry, add a background – I've mixed white, blue and sienna for a soft grey.

CUTTING IN TO ADD GLITCHES

You can then use the same background mix to cut into the subject using elongated blocks, lines and dabs. Experiment with marks to see what looks most effective. This will be down to personal taste and will make you appreciate using abstract marks.

- *Vary the sizes and length of the marks or use different brushes and pressures.*
- *Try using palette knives or cards to apply the mix.*
- *Reverse the process by including colours from the subject in the background.*

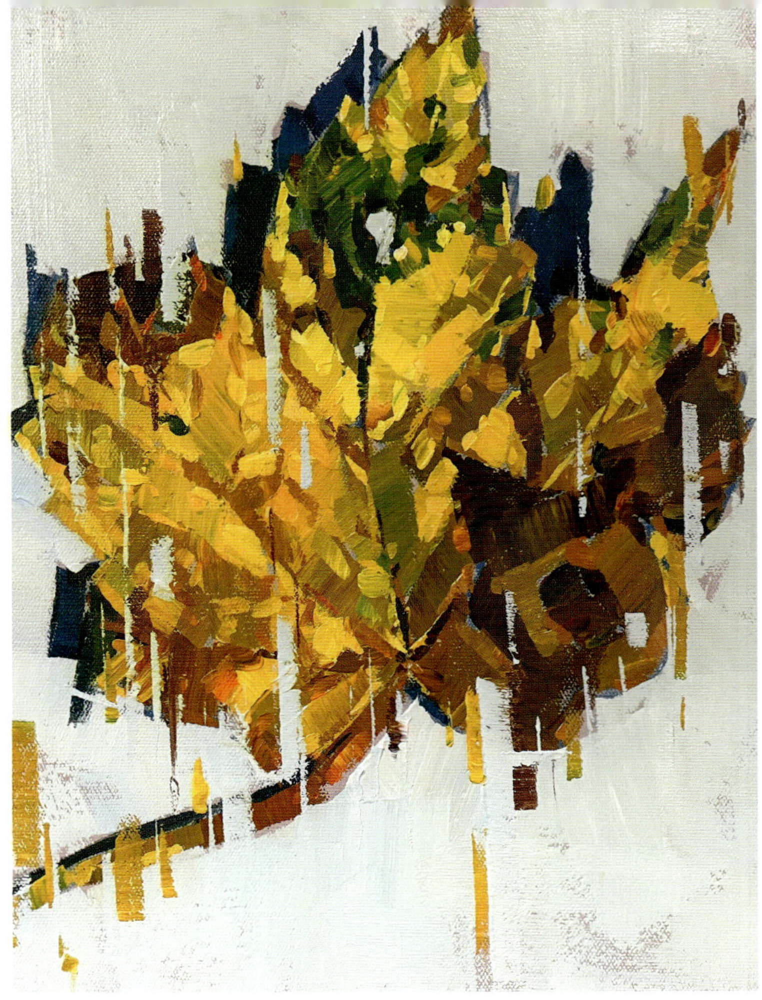

IMPERFECTION ADDS IMPACT

Contemporary artists tend to look for more than simply replicating what they see, so a talent for drawing and painting realistically is sometimes not enough. Glitches can turn impressive but unengaging representational art into something much more striking – imperfection is more interesting!

Playing with size

A lot of the digital images we view nowadays tend to be small thumbnails or fragments of detail from a larger image. Thumbnails are made up of big shapes of tone or colour and the details are minimal.

When scrolling social media accounts or viewing artwork online, you might skip through a multitude of great artworks because they just don't grab you when reduced to the size of a postage stamp. As this becomes a norm for judging images, try incorporating this concept into your artwork by applying the big shapes and contrasts of a small thumbnail to a full-size artwork.

THE THUMBNAIL APPROACH

The next time you find a thumbnail image that packs a punch, save it so you can use the colour scheme or tones for your next artwork. It won't matter if the theme is completely different – you're simply borrowing the look to mimic the impact.

The colour scheme I've chosen (above right) is high impact, and I've chosen to use it to paint a subject (below right) that is much more drably-coloured in reality – fine at full size, but hardly eye-catching as a small image.

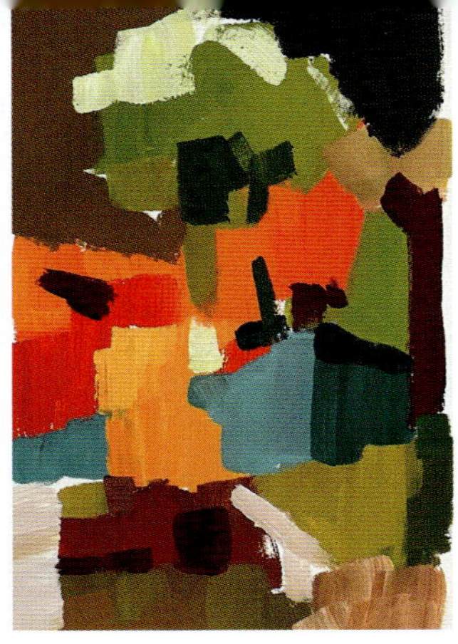

COLOUR SCHEME VISUAL

Inspired by an artwork I found online, I made a visual sketch of the main 'beats' of colours and how they were balanced compositionally.

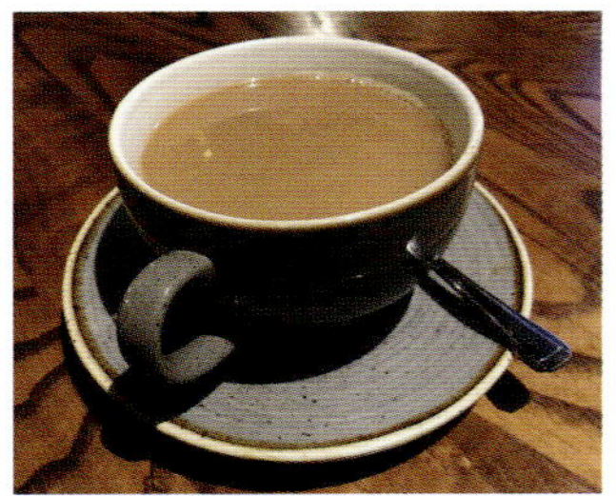

SUBJECT

I took this photograph of my cup of tea in a café. It's fairly mundane but an interesting colour scheme and painting it at a huge size will make it much more dynamic.

THE TECHNIQUE

Clean applications provide illuminated colour. As more information is added, these clean applications can get diluted, so be sparing with the marks you add, or it'll stop looking like a thumbnail. Compare the visual with the final artwork to see how the impact is retained.

Keep some areas underworked, allowing the purity of the initial colour to come through. When adding additional marks or detail, apply them with confidence – avoid fuss!

Adjust on the fly to account for differences in orientation: this landscape-format artwork is based on a portrait-format colour scheme.

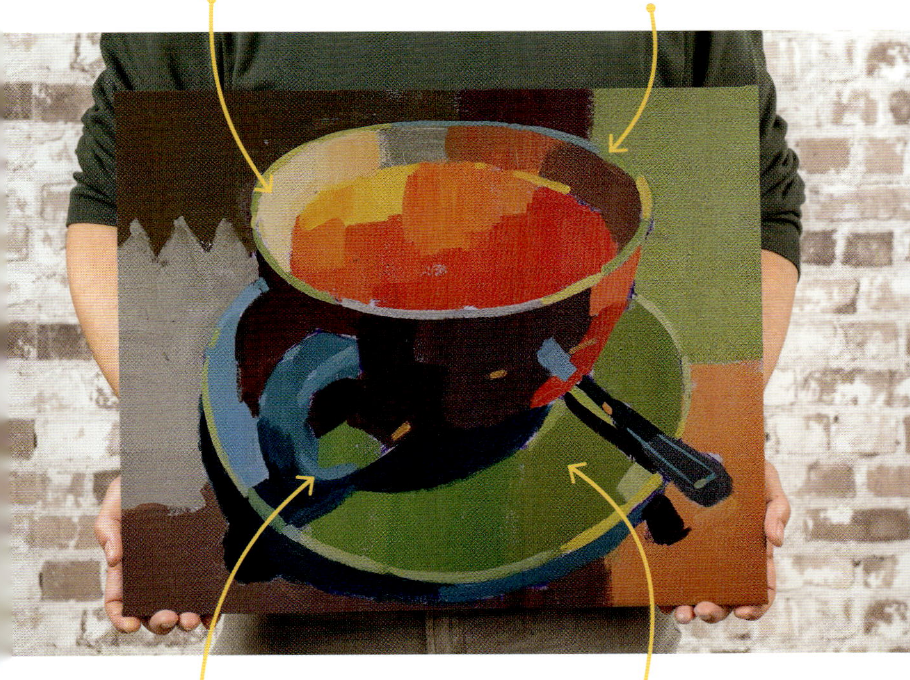

Working on a light grey base colour, I used a flat brush to block in the same colours used in the visual. I added white to create softer tints where the visual guide provides these colour cues.

Note that I have not used all the colours from the visual, and have added additional subtle shades to suit the image.

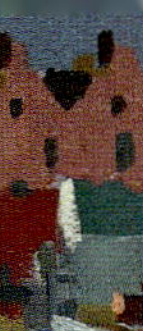

One-session painting

Here's an exercise that provides the best results when painting with acrylics: painting a scene – or at least the main statements – in one go. This is similar to the traditional practice known as *alla prima*. With this approach, you are aiming to make your choice of colours, lighting and where to place the large shapes. You'll allow these layers to dry before applying those final details along with strengthening some light and colour.

It's difficult painting over several sittings, as identifying and accurately recreating colour mixes is tricky, which slows the process. The spontaneity of an in-depth painting session will keep you in the loop of colours used, while the speedy process will help make your mark-making more concise.

Get a lot painted early

Get your materials ready, begin with a sketch if needed, and – most importantly – use a large mixing tray. I always recommend large brushes initially for coverage, but they're great for mixing large pools of colour.

When you start painting, make a conscious effort to increase your pace as you mix colour and apply it, and try to make quick decisions rather than over-think things. The pools of colours you create on the mixing tray will become invaluable over the course of the session.

Once you're finished, take a break and come back with fresh eyes to add your finishing touches – these will be much more enjoyable with the basis of the painting firmly in place.

Why is using a large mixing tray key?

Acrylics dry quickly, but if you're generous with the amount of paint you use, the mixes you make on your tray will remain useable throughout the painting, becoming an extension of your palette beyond the pure wells of colour. These mixes will create a consistent look to the painting and be used to bridge new colours that you introduce into your artwork.

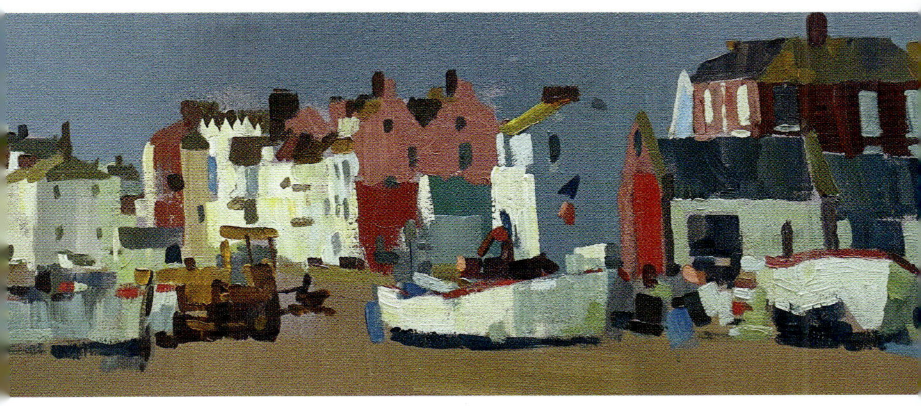

ALDEBURGH BEACH – AFTER ONE SESSION

The scene here was painted in one go, taking only short breaks. This approach was particularly helpful in ensuring consistency between the reds: mixing the light tints and shades of red from a common pool on the palette was invaluable.

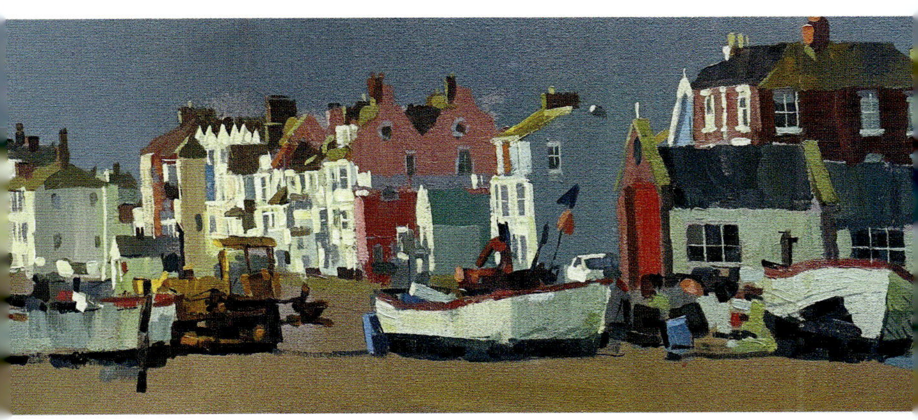

REFINEMENTS, DARKS AND LIGHTS

This finished version was polished off in a subsequent painting session. It contains a few stronger darks, heightened lights and some refinement of details – all of which were made much easier by having the broad strokes properly and quickly established.

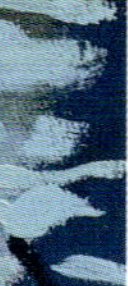

Taking your time

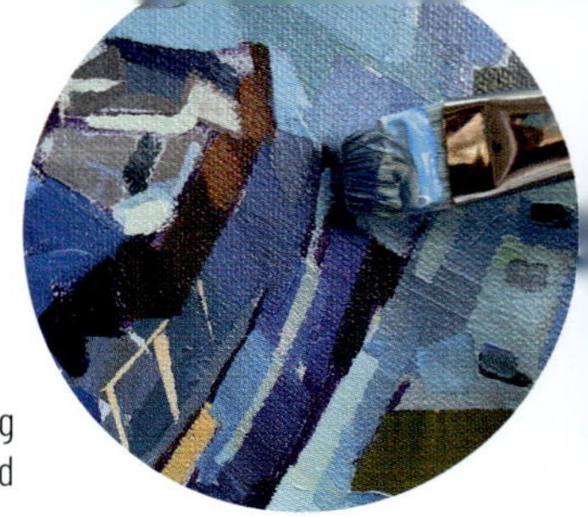

When you do have a large, time-consuming project, the best way to work through it is to break it up so you have a definite beginning, middle and end. I associate it with running a marathon: start off slow and easy, build up a momentum and end with a sprint.

Steady start Start with big, bold, overall shapes to create a general feel, then begin to work through all the information at a steady pace.

Pacemaking Keep a steady pace through the middle section. It's a long haul working in sections, but is also rewarding as every inch of the artwork is considered.

Sprint finish Refining at the end is potentially the most problematic stage, focusing on details can result in tunnel vision. Don't get caught up in spending days fiddling. When you reach the end stages, create a deadline. Keep moving along relatively quickly; stand back as much as you can to survey the impact of details you add. The fewer refinements you make, the more exciting marks you'll keep from earlier.

WHICH BRUSH?

At the start, the paint is applied almost neat, in one or two blocky strokes of a flat brush.

Refinements such as rigging on boats or dabs of highlights are added at the end, using smaller brushes.

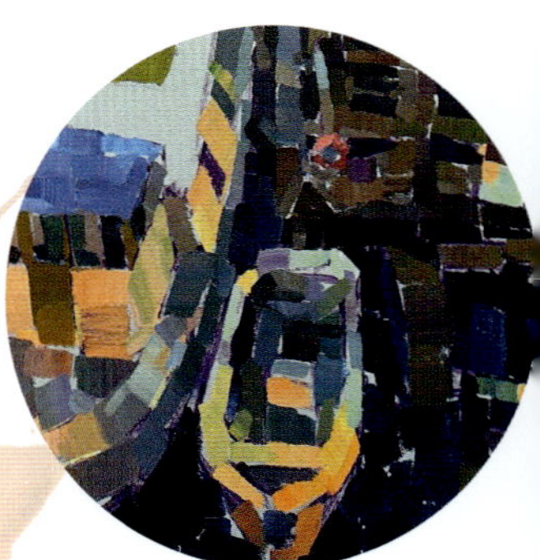

UNREFINED

During the early stages, avoid the temptation to finish sections off – aim only to establish the colour and tones in that area.

Work quickly where you can

Spending more time on a painting doesn't necessarily translate into a better result. You may get a more polished finish, and avoid the technical issues that can arise from working quickly, but speedy paintings are more enjoyable, as you have less thinking time and they encourage an instinctive response. This usually translates into more lively results.

BRIDGE AT NIGHT

Three to four full days is a good deadline for large paintings like this, which
measures 76 x 61cm (30 x 24in); any longer and you risk losing interest.

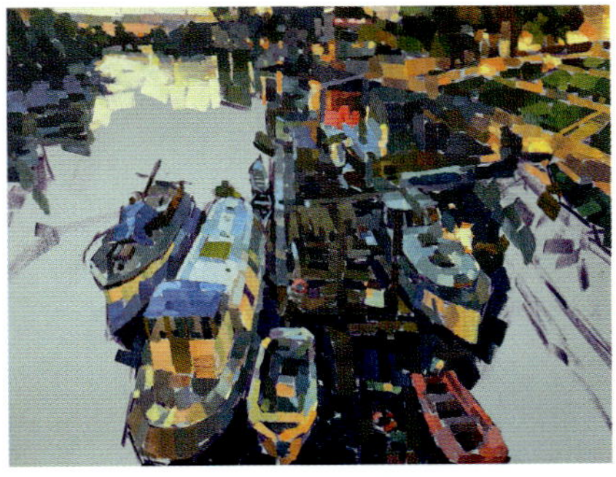

BEGINNING

*Working on a grey base colour, roughly
sketch out the scene, beginning the
painting by working up various sections.*

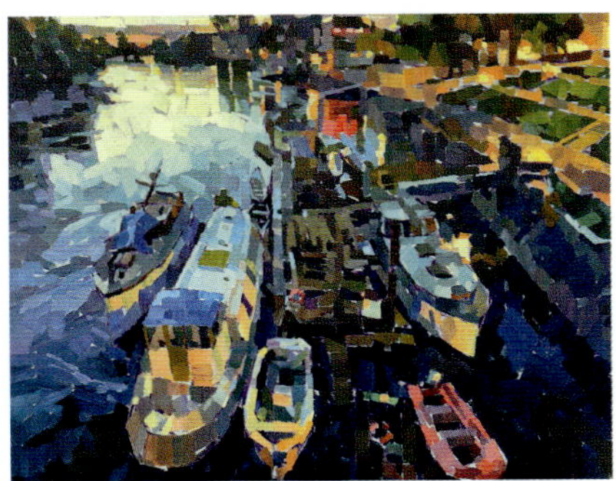

MIDDLE

*Work in sections, maintain your discipline,
and keep track of the colours you use.*

*Flagging interest in a painting will show
through your brush marks becoming
repetitive, and the colours becoming more
generic and less nuanced. To avoid this,
work to your self-imposed time limit, as this
will keep up the pace.*

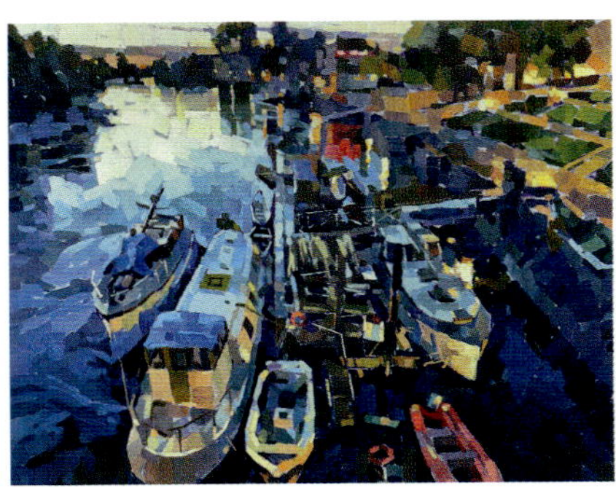

END

*Once everything is covered and an overall
balance achieved, use stronger darks
and lights, along with some touches of
saturated colour, to 'crisp up' the image.*

*As acrylics dry darker, you'll see the
profound differences a spark of light tint
creates. Allow applications to dry off to
gauge the true effect.*

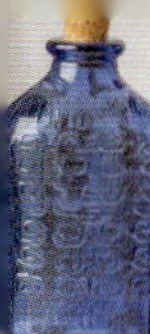

Painting the everyday

If you're ever at a loss for something to paint, just look around. The most mundane objects can provide invaluable resource material for an artist – and all the better if it resonates personally with you. This practice takes the obscure and places it on a pedestal.

Before picking up your phone to browse for inspiration, stop and look around. Look around your house, studio or surroundings, and take note of how the shadows fall in your kitchen on a sunny afternoon; the swirl of your favourite hot drink in the evening; a hastily stacked spice rack... Perhaps a couple of items which are so familiar that they have become overlooked will now catch your eye. Use these as your source material for a painting.

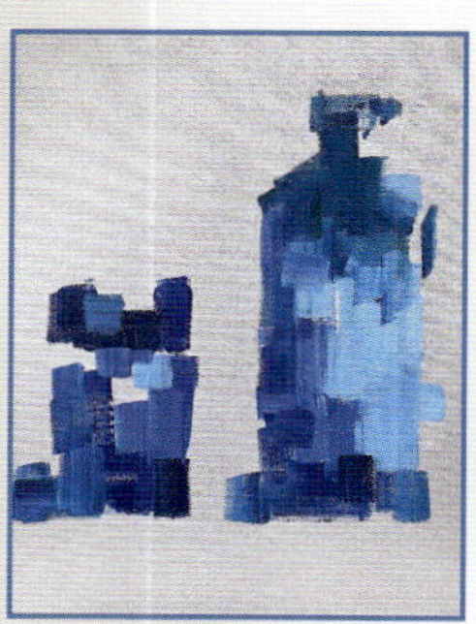

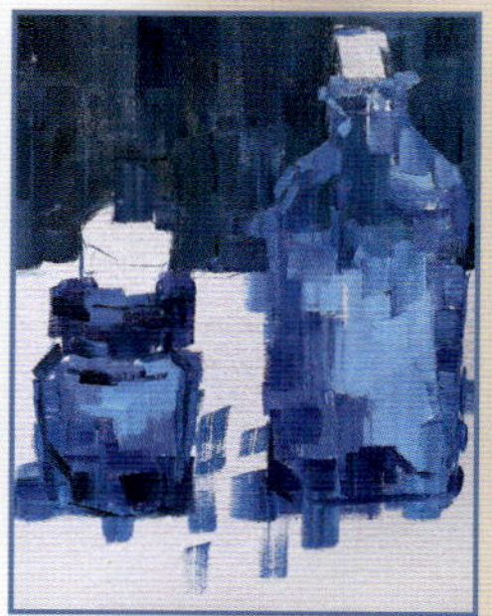

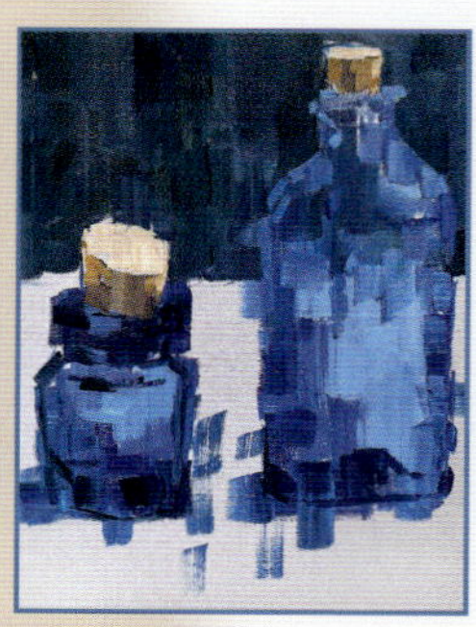

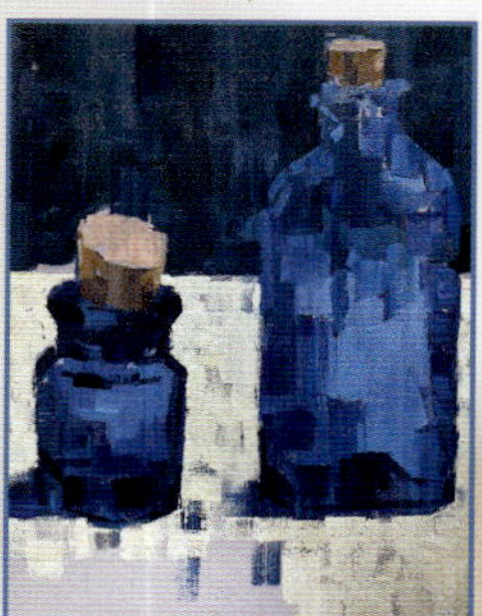

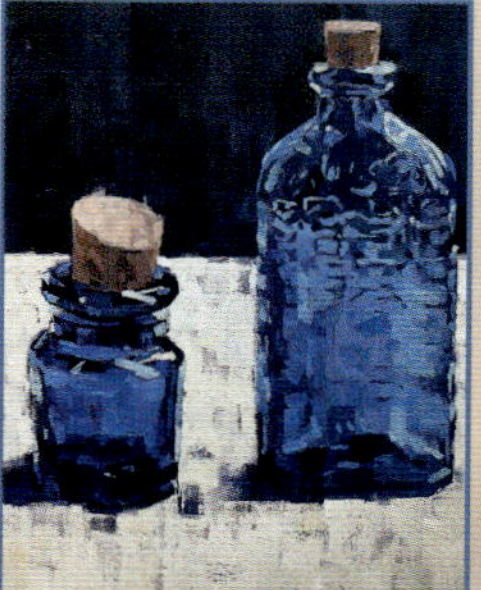

BLUE BOTTLES

The moment you try to arrange the scene too much it will start to look planned – where possible, paint the scene just as you find it. The more uncontrived the arrangement, the more authentic the feel.

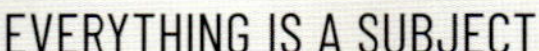

EVERYTHING IS A SUBJECT

It is a really valuable lesson that everything is a potential subject to paint. Some themes might need an extra boost in lighting or additional elements added to create dynamism. Here are some ideas to get you started with the practice of looking close to home for ideas:

- A bowl of crisps to go with your hot chocolate as a still life.
- Dig out a favourite battered old toy, and look at it with fresh eyes.
- Take a couple of photographs on your commute or regular walking route, and use them to paint or draw from.

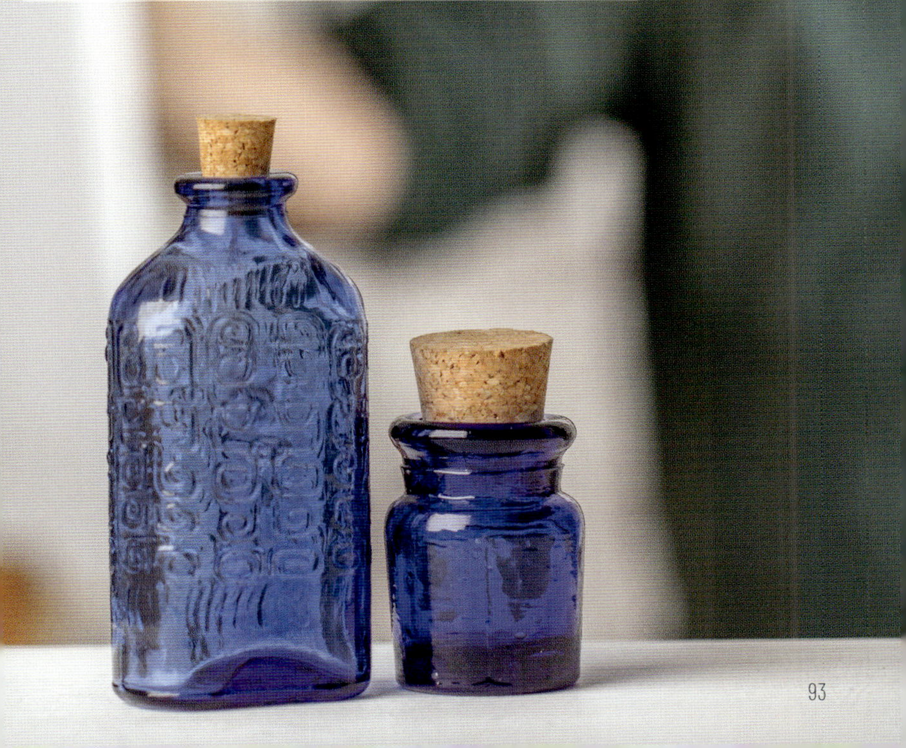

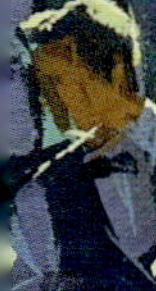

Café scenes

To tackle complex scenes, look for outlines: we respond to a good silhouette more than the elements that make up the shape.

Suggest For busy scenes, start by sketching out the main elements, paying particular attention to how light carves out interesting shapes against darks. Treat the early stages as a blocking-in exercise, melding large areas together rather than separating them into individual shapes. This immediately creates a cohesive mass.

Define Once the main forms are established with some suggestion of certain colours, mix up plenty of white with lemon yellow and light blue. A bit more care is required to cut into the lights especially around the figures.

I've painted the lights using different-sized blocks with some jagged linework. These crisp edges create a contrast with the larger areas of relatively flat colour and tone that I began with. I also use neat acrylic to make the paint pop and dominate the early layers.

Refine I use softer tints and colours elaborating on cups, glasses, faces and arms. I add additional details for the areas around the figures.

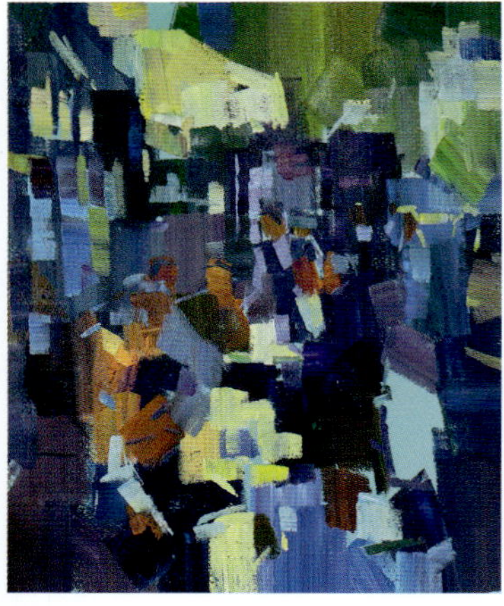

STAGE 1 Look for the silhouette of figures, cars or buildings, not the information within them. Block in colour and meld some of the shapes together.

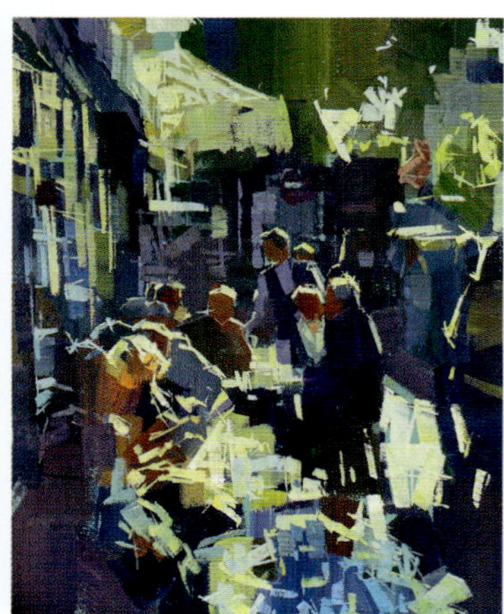

STAGE 2 Use strong lights to define the figures, this is mainly white, lemon yellow and light blue.

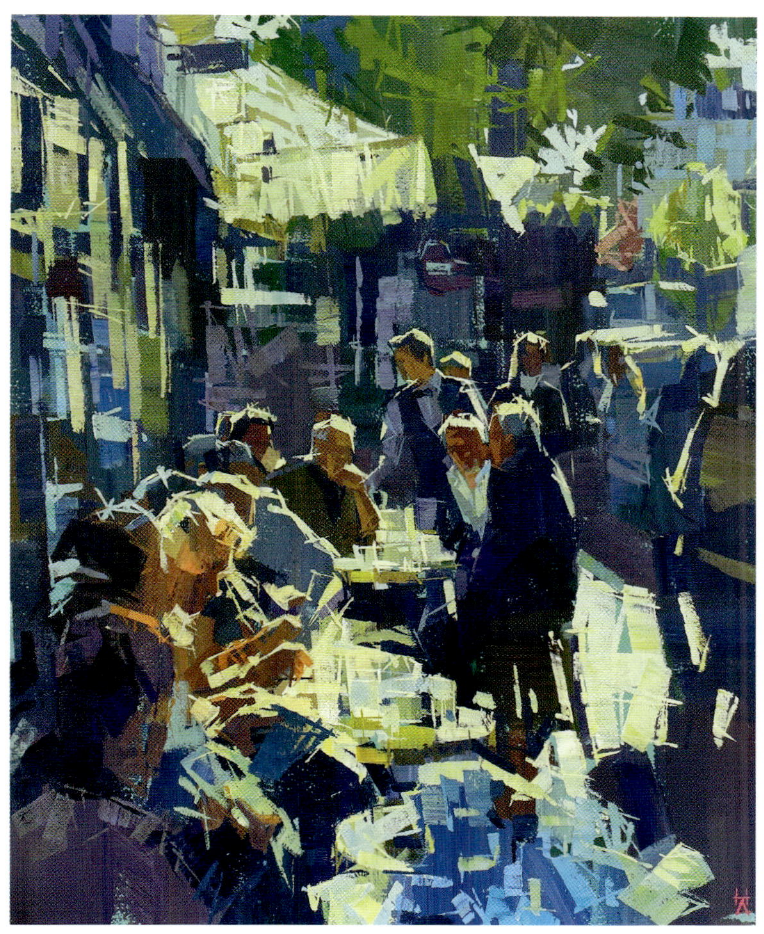

THE FINISHED PAINTING

Subtle tints are used to bring out faces, the café façade and areas behind. Keep the silhouettes crisp and the painting will be easier to read.

Animals

Add some 'wild life' to your wildlife – when it comes to painting animals, try to avoid the fluffy, cute depictions that humanize the subject.

MATCH YOUR APPROACH TO THE SUBJECT

Instead of refined, blended brush work, try exposed blocks of colour and use neat paint for impasto effects. Weighty paint creates a tactile look that's great for contouring the shape of this elephant.

Finer marks are reserved for the focal point – the head.

The strong light behind contains very light blue and lemon yellow for a bit of fizz.

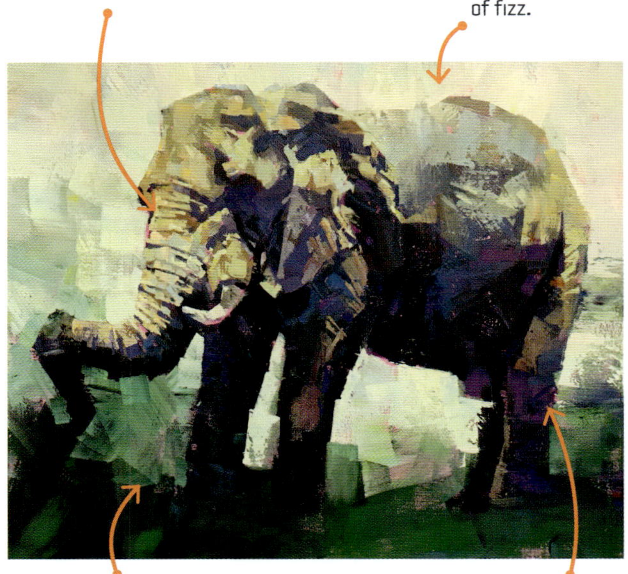

A blurred, sketchy background retains key information and lends weight – but doesn't distract from the animal.

Along with the greys you might expect, note the use of violet and blues to lift the colour.

FROM PHOTOGRAPH TO PAINTING

Wildlife photography brings high-definition realism to the subject, capturing every nuance of detail or moody tone – not all of which is desirable. Lose the background so the animal can take centre stage.

Try adding splatter marks, using a single background colour, incorporating abstract swirls, using blocky brushstrokes or bringing in contrasting light effects.

SIMPLIFY FOR EFFECT

Instead of the enclosure in the source photograph (right), I used an almost bleached light behind the rhino and a burning orange light under it to symbolize loss of habitat – this adds an arresting narrative to the painting.

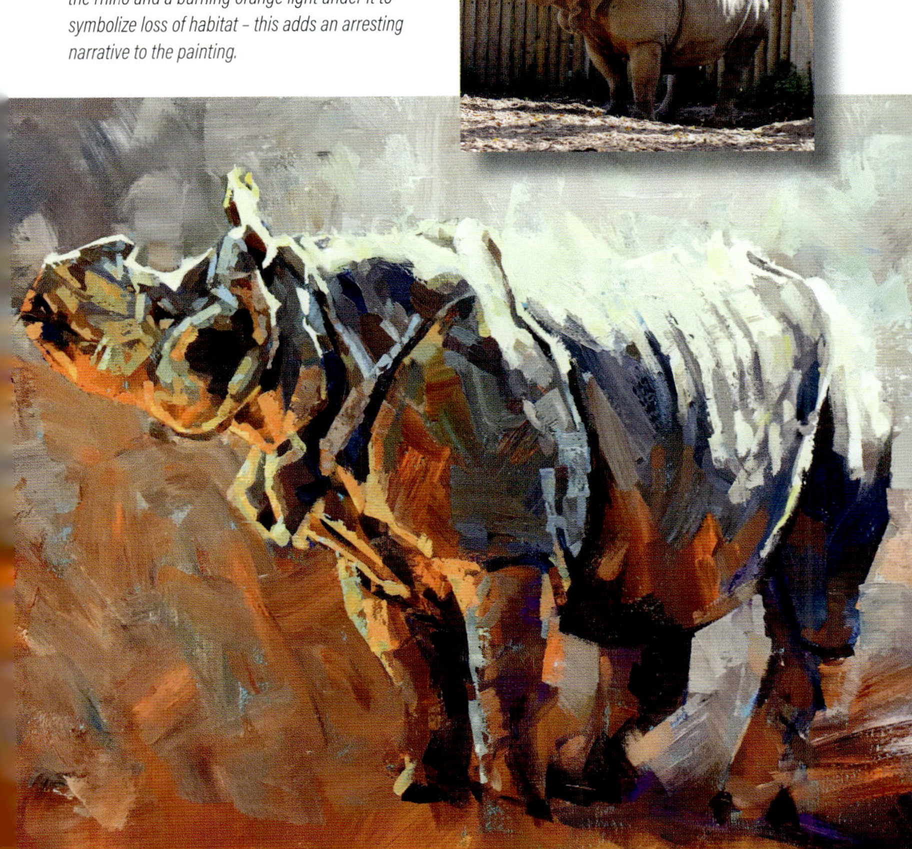

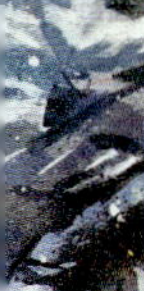

Night scenes

Night scenes are incredibly underrated as a subject to paint – there's so much on offer for the artist, including multiple coloured light sources, the lines of the shadows shooting off in all directions, and elements framed by contrasting darks and lights. This painting of St Pancras Station, King's Cross in London at night showcases how effective night scenes can be.

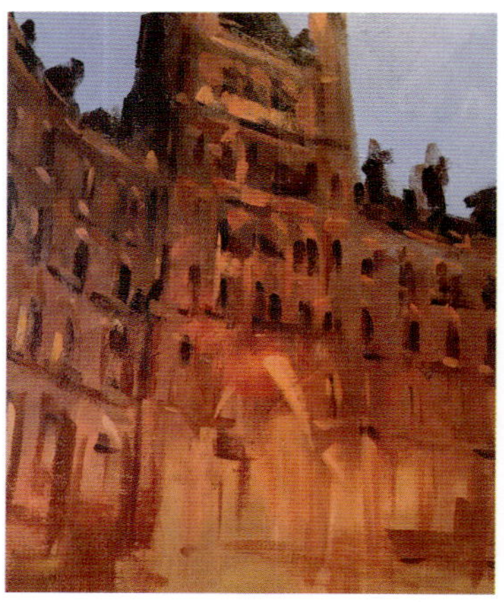

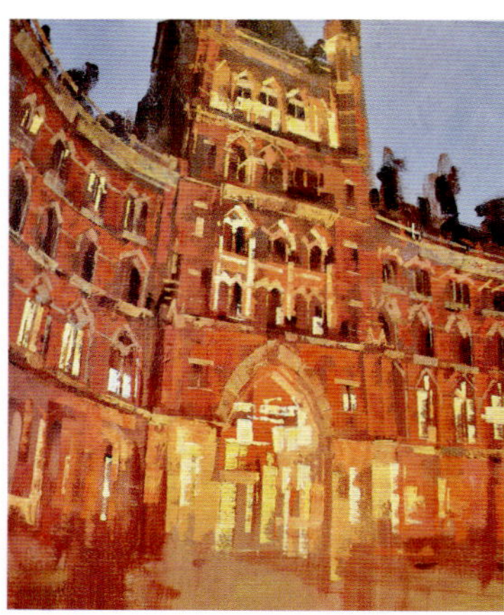

STAGE 1 Working over a base colour of light ochre, paint the flat blue sky using a mix of cobalt blue, burnt sienna and white. Fill in the building with burnt red mid-tone mixes of red, ochre, violet and dabs of blue; adding more yellow for the main doorway. Apply these layers using a thick wash, diluting the paint to a cream consistency using flow improver and water to allow for some blending. Place the architectural features using a darker version of the burnt red.

STAGE 2 Switch to using card squeegees (see pages 28–29) to apply details. Prepare a range of light-tinted yellows and ochre mixed with white, along with mid-toned burnt orange and deep reds for the brickwork. Starting at the top with strong yellows, define the arched windows by picking up colour on the squeegees and applying it in lines and blocks.

Wipe the card with a damp tissue
after every few strokes to help
make consistent marks.

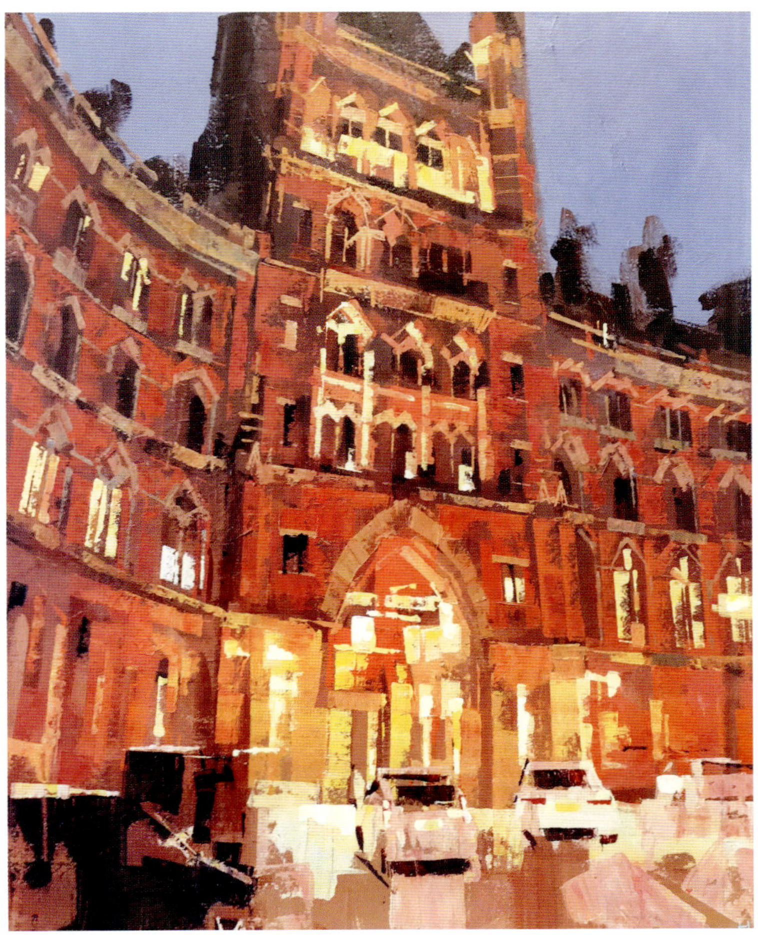

STAGE 3 Dark tones are brought forward using violet, Prussian blue and burnt sienna. More white is added to yellow for stronger lights used at the main doorway with additional elements of the cars added at the end.

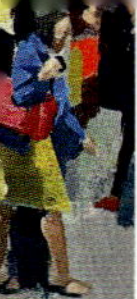

Busy streets

Paintings of street scenes can become very busy and cluttered. You would usually leave some information out of a painting to make it very clear to the viewer what's important – but this can be tricky in urban scenes, as you need a sense of bustle and busyness to ensure the street looks lively and interesting.

BALANCE OF CONTRAST

The answer is to use soft pastel-tinted areas to create calm empty space, and contrast them with extreme darks and shots of rich colour to create focal points. You can create pastel tints simply by adding white to your mixes.

In the examples shown opposite, the aim was to create large flat areas and a line of frenetic activity. Almost all of the colours for the sky and buildings include white, while the street level contains plenty of contrasting rich mixes made with strong saturated paint.

For the extreme contrasts, I even mixed pure black with rich reds and yellows to link colour with the extremes of tone.

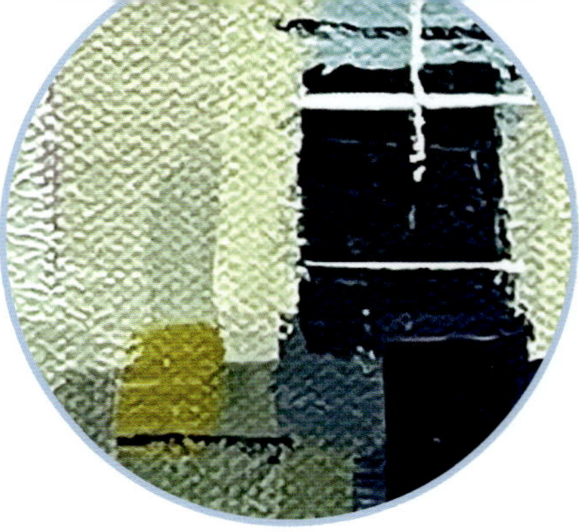

Strive for contrast

Extreme contrasts between dark tones and pastel soft tints are the key.

OUT OF THE STREETS

When introducing particular ideas into your artwork you'll begin creating a style or consistency that gives your work a look that's unique to you. Try this technique for landscapes and figures – you'll be struck by the effects created by contrasting pastel tints with bold saturated mixes.

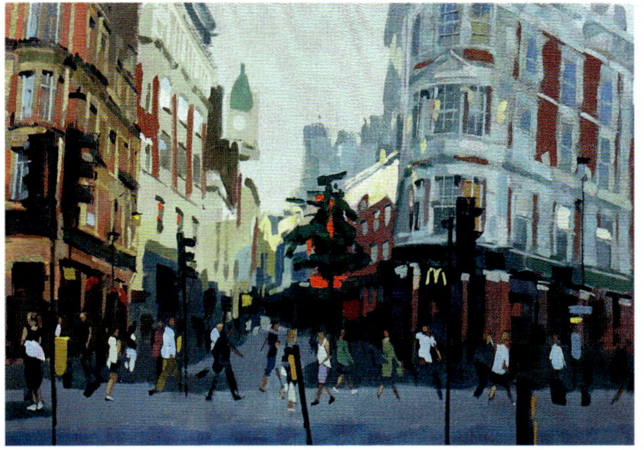

When employing these techniques for street scenes, the traditionally hard surface of the buildings become soft against the sprawling life below – which in turn contains all the strong tones and colour.

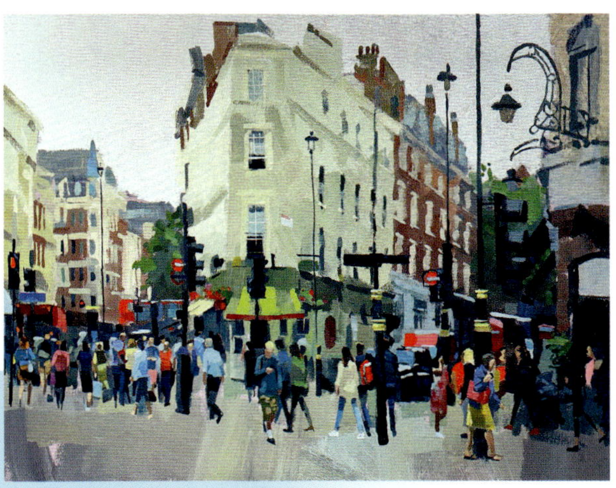

The flat open sky here creates calm space. The tops of buildings are rendered softly as they reach skywards – which makes it easier to draw immediate focal points from the street level. Look at the pure colour, bright lights and earthy tones in the crowd.

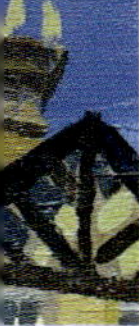

Buildings with character

Older buildings tend to have more personality than newer ones, as they've been weatherbeaten, and historical architectural styles tended to be more ornate.

While the greater use of glass or metals in new builds can create interesting reflections, the main challenge we face in producing an interesting street scene is their stark nature. Figures can bring animation to a street scene, but if their presence doesn't fit your picture, you're left with the problem that a lot of modern buildings are simply dull – little more than glorified boxes. How can we make them more interesting?

RELAX AND LOOSEN UP

- Try starting without an outline and go straight in with paint: block in the general shapes, looking for subtle variations of colour in the structure.
- When painting buildings in acrylics, avoid being overly precise. The moment you tense up your lines or marks, you'll lose energy – they'll be sharp, perhaps accurate, but they'll lack personality.
- Multiple lines, even accurate ones, create both clutter and an overall monotonous look. Unless you're working as an architect, start by using wobbly lines or edges.
- Relax your painting arm as this will translate in the edges you paint. If the lines are a bit shaky, learn to live with it – as more appear there will be a consistent look to these marks.

BRINGING OUT THE CHARACTER

This hotel has a number of interesting features, along with strong contrasting light. We need to bring this character out without making the result clinical or overly technical.

The tone and colour helps to create a representational image, and while it's important that the perspective of the building generally makes sense, you don't need to be precise. Here, holding a ruler to any lines shows the characterful 'flaws'.

BIG, BOLD SHADOWS

Adding large shadows like this will immediately create form.

KEEP AN EYE ON THE BIGGER PICTURE

Some lines are left out altogether while detail is played down to allow breathing space. Compare how the characterful beams are included while the tiling on the roof is rendered very simply.

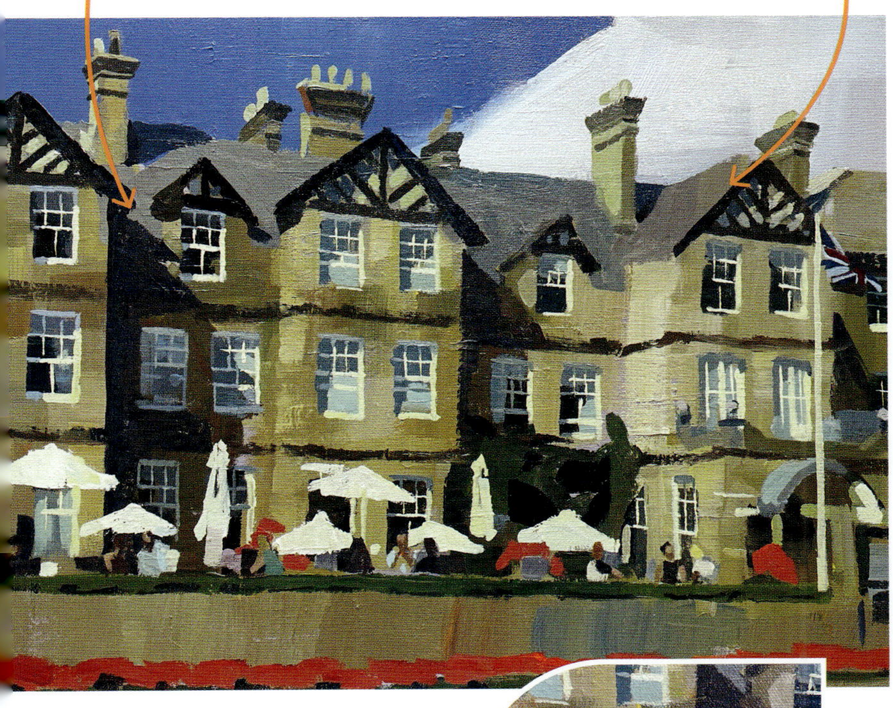

DETAILS

Finer details help to give a sense of detail. Add them after the big shapes, but don't include any frame work. Save more intense drawing like the lines for the window frames until right at the end. Use a couple of smaller flat brushes for this – and deliberately allow the lines to sway a little.

Composing portraits

Social media has changed the way we look at contemporary portraiture. The portability of camera phones makes for more interesting, informal compositions. Filters and effects break from naturalism into more abstract territory. Facial expressions and poses are more animated, creating less formality. For the artist there's still the technical challenges of simply painting or drawing, but it's worth considering these new possibilities when composing a portrait.

MOVE IT

Move the portrait to one side of the other, rather than centralizing it. This creates more spatial drama than a perfectly centred pose.

Try having the figure looking away, or even partly cropped out of the scene. You could try tilting the angle or even looking down onto the figure.

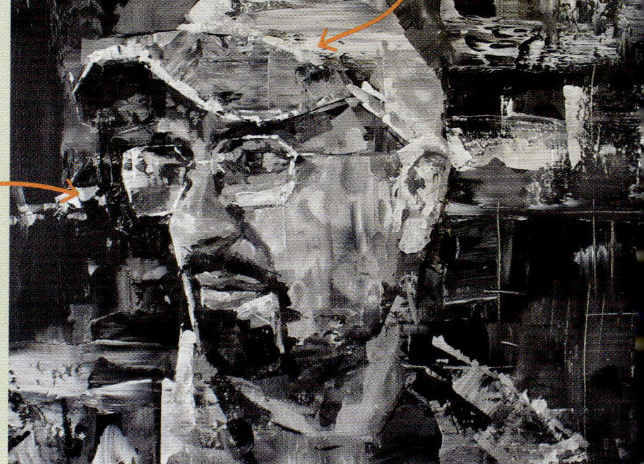

A hat breaks the subject's profile, adding dramatic angles.

Accessories can be useful: a pair of glasses create sparkly highlights and reflections of what we don't see.

CROP IN OR OUT

Traditional portraits are non-confrontational, the sitter set back to reveal their environment or elements that reflect their interests. I prefer the intimacy of cropping in, as this encourages the viewer to fully engage with the portrait.

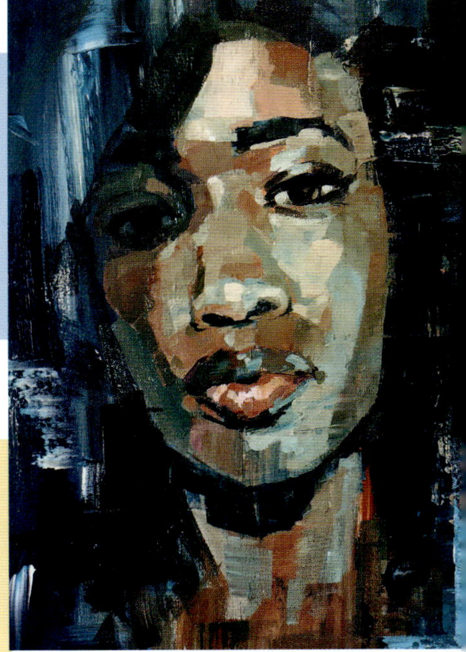

HAIR

Hair can be a great prop for portraits. The style or colour can initiate more saturated colour, several colours in some cases, while the length creates dynamic diagonals leading into the portrait.

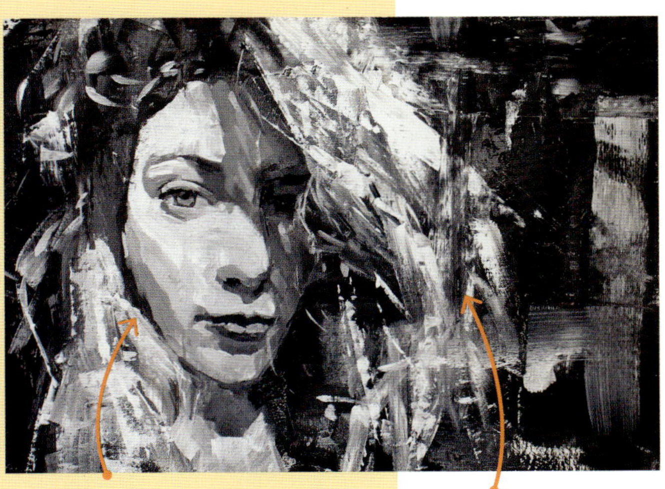

Frenetic brushwork in the hair contrasts with the steady, controlled facial features.

Varying tonal values in the hair contour and frame the face.

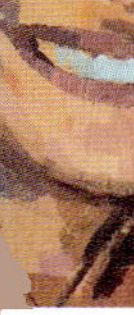

Portraits on commission

There's no getting round it – painting a portrait for someone is a real challenge. There's already an expectation of a likeness – or if you're stylizing the portrait, a clear character trait. Here are some tips that'll help you strike a good compromise between personal expression and accuracy.

STAGE 1 We're aiming for expressive marks – but also a likeness. Start the painting with a turquoise base colour, and add a simple outline once dry. Following the colours from the reference photograph closely, apply blocks of neat acrylics.

At this stage, the faces are left simply as areas of flat colour.

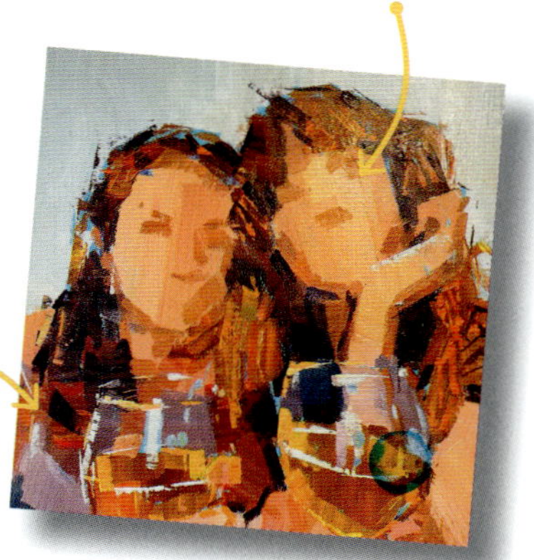

Before the acrylic dries, drag some paint into the background to break up edges and disrupt lines.

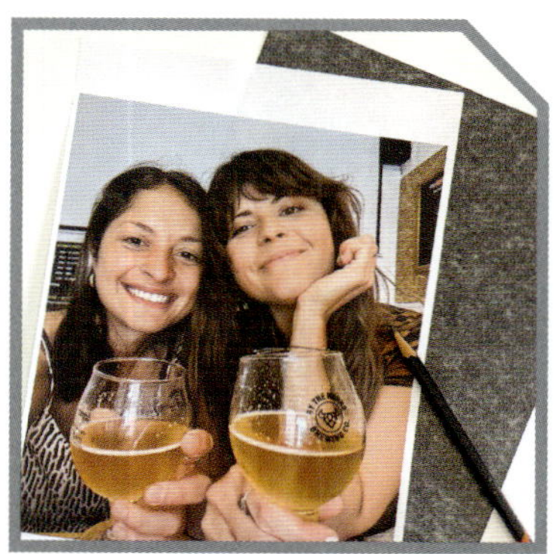

TRACE AND PAINT

I rarely use tracings in artwork, but when you need the portraits to be as accurate as possible, it's a great additional tool.

Place carbon paper on your painting surface, place the picture on top, and then use a pencil to draw round the outline and main shapes – the pressure will transfer carbon from the paper to the surface. Once the image is on the painting surface, work from it with plenty of care and attention.

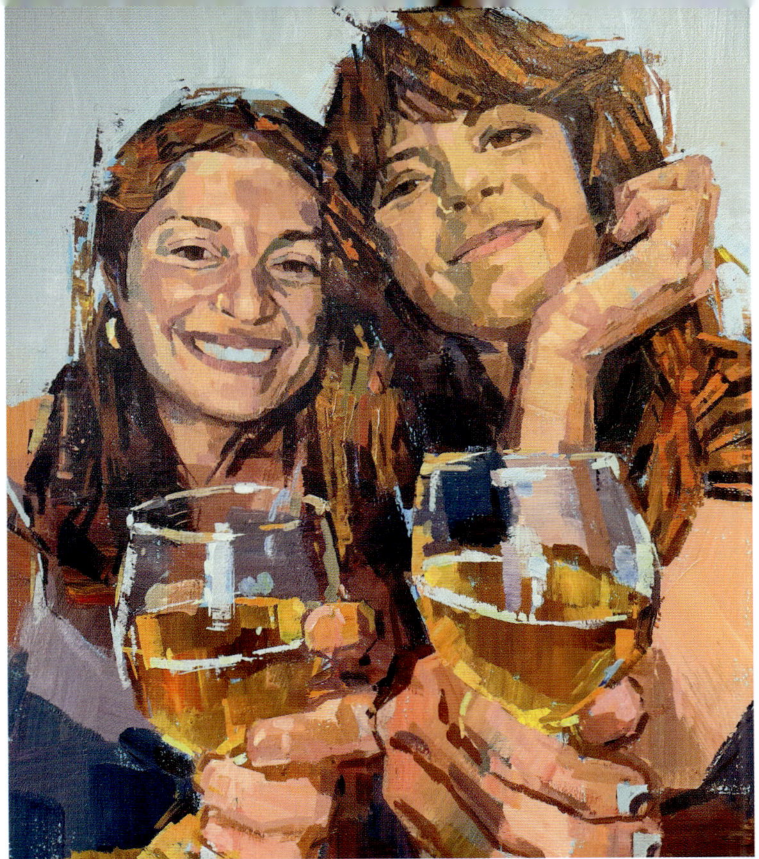

STAGE 2 Once dry, print out the reference photograph to a size that corresponds with the space left for the portraits to provide an accurate outline of the features. It's then back to painting, where I use similar shades, tones and tints already used to match the portraits.

THE IMPORTANCE OF REFERENCE

It's key to work from good reference material: a clear photograph and consideration for lighting will make your task much easier.

Take your own photographs if you can, steering away from huge smiles, which distort the face and add lines, or the head leaning back, which gives undue emphasis to the nostrils.

Painting water

Certain subjects, such as water, may seem easier to paint with other mediums – oils would provide you with more time to blend, while watercolour would create fluid, organic effects simply by dropping the paint on a wet surface.

Luckily, acrylics also have their own unique strengths, including their incredible versatility. Here's an exercise that will help you to achieve a sense of movement while also retaining those all-important nuances of colours when portraying water.

LAYING THE GROUNDWORK

In this example, a large percentage of the reflective, watery effects can be painted early on. These initial applications are to lay the large groundwork of colours, light and movement.

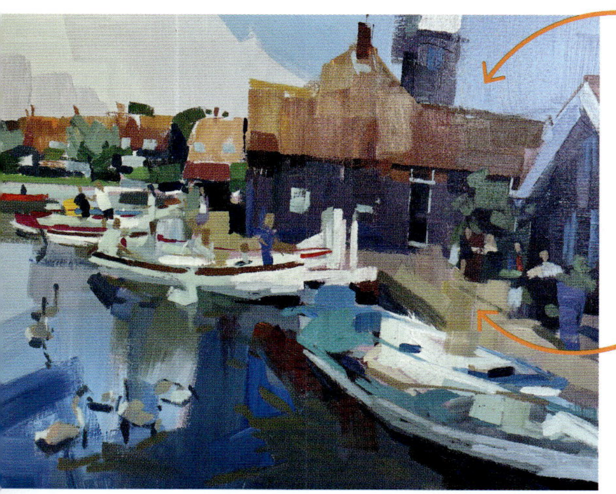

NEAT PAINT, CLEAN MARKS

Use a large flat brush with plenty of relatively neat paint – though you might want to add a little water if it's a large painting.

AIM FOR VARIETY

Vary the colours within areas by adding some white, some darker tones and some richer colour.

DON'T OVER-DETAIL

Look out for shadows, reflections from boats or changes of colours – aim for an almost abstract impression of the scene.

BUILT FOR SPEED

Using acrylics will mean the early layers dry quickly, so there's little risk of paint bleeding where you don't want it.

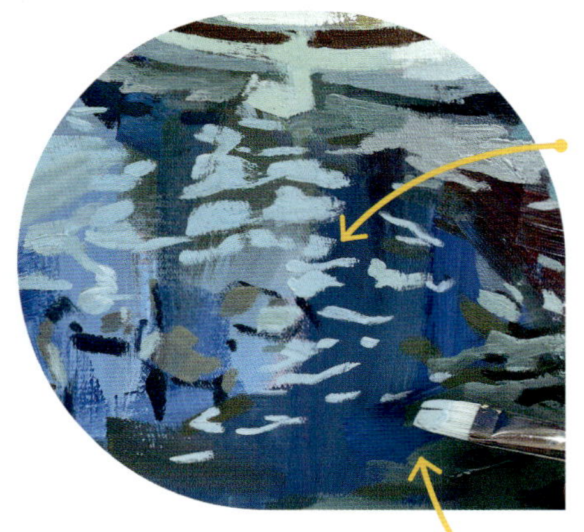

COLOURS

The opaque nature of acrylics makes judging colour easier. I used white with blues, a touch of lemon yellow, and red oxide to 'grey off' the blues. I've varied these tints by adding green or ochre to the overall mix. Nothing is blended; these strokes simply sit on the first layer.

ATMOSPHERE, NOT REPRODUCTION

Avoid adding every ripple you can see: you're conveying a feel for the water, rather than copying the scene.

CHOPPY MID-SIZE MARKS

Use a mid-size brush to add ripples, as this will create the surface movement and contrast against larger marks. Going down a brush size later will create crisper marks.

FLEXIBILITY

Shadows and highlights can be added at any stage with acrylics – there's no need to consider the layers underneath. For the final polish, this meant I could add darker or mid-toned ripples along with some tinkles of stronger light.

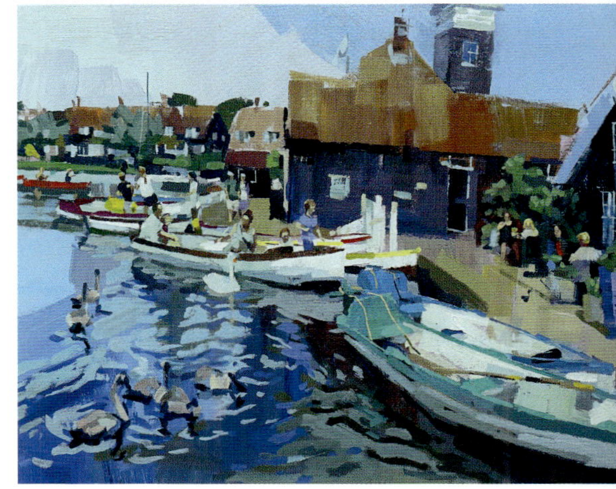

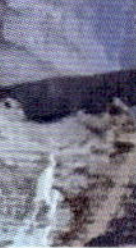

Painting a series

Working on a series of paintings will help to create a distinctive unified look, and will also reinforce the ideas you want to get across to the viewer. The number of paintings in the series can vary, but between four and a dozen is a good number to aim for.

As long as the theme and style remain at least somewhat consistent across the series, you can experiment to your heart's content.

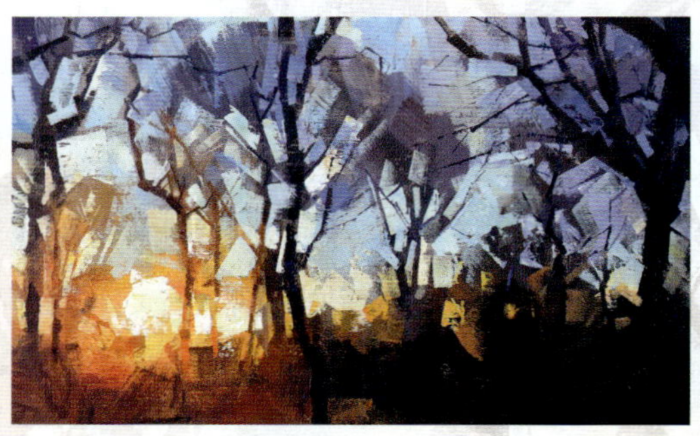

The series of five small-scale tree artworks shown across these pages are consistent in style and theme. This has allowed me to experiment with the colour palette and energy of the brushwork, while still producing paintings that clearly relate to each other.

WHAT MAKES A SERIES?

For an effective series, you need to balance variety with some consistent elements. If you vary your styles or themes too much in a series it can look disjointed and unfocused, so concentrate on developing a single theme within the series. This could be a particular subject such as street scenes or trees, or based on something more ephemeral – feelings, perhaps, or the effects of light.

There's a great feeling of satisfaction when a series is complete; you'll be left brimming with ideas for your next one.

You might link the paintings in your series through marks, colours or tone; through using one medium or a particular variety. You might paint one element – such as focal figures – in a particular consistent way, while the environments they inhabit could be wildly different.

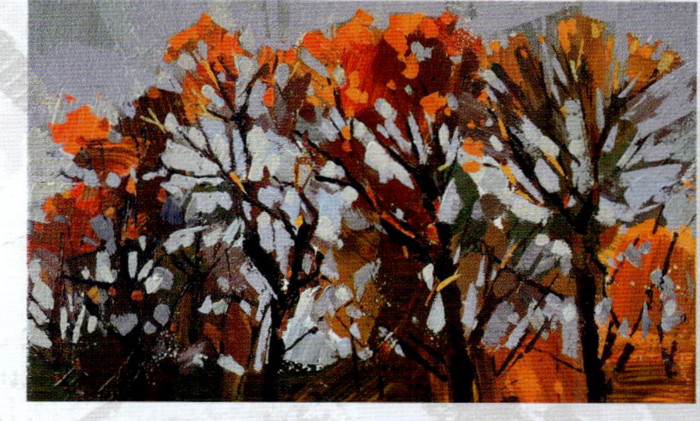

HINTS AND TIPS

Once you have a goal of producing a series of artworks, there's a few things to consider:

- Keep the same proportions to create a sense of continuity and reinforce the connection between the pieces.

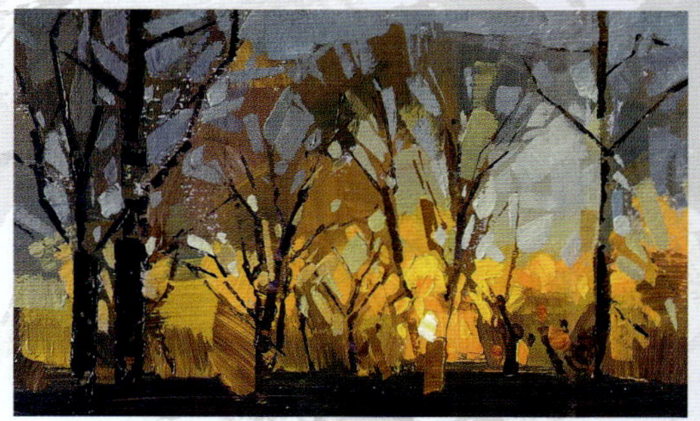

- A deadline will help prevent you overthinking or constantly 'pecking' at the paintings.

- Aim at an overall standard. It's better to have a consistent quality than one great piece with several lacklustre ones. Assume a couple will fall short of what you hoped for and plan to paint a few extras.

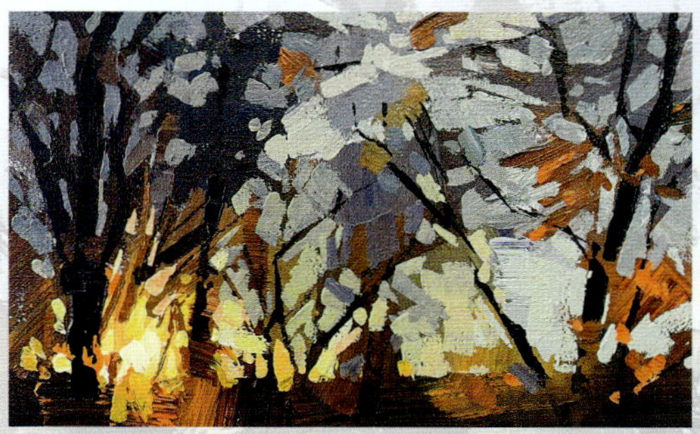

- Find an outlet for the work, whether in an gallery exhibition or online.

- Link the series with the same style of frame for continuity – you might also paint on the same-sized canvas or paper.

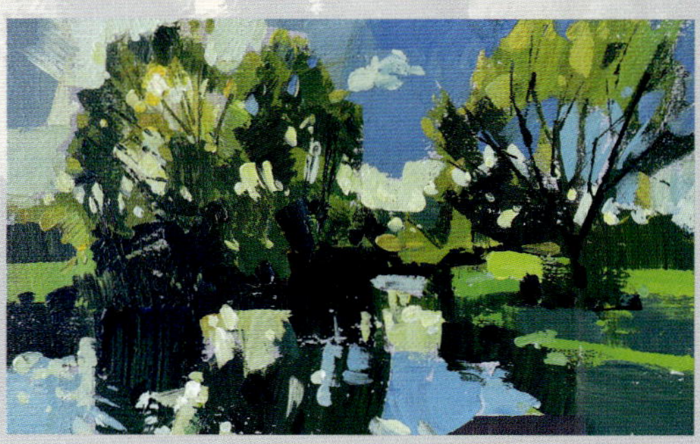

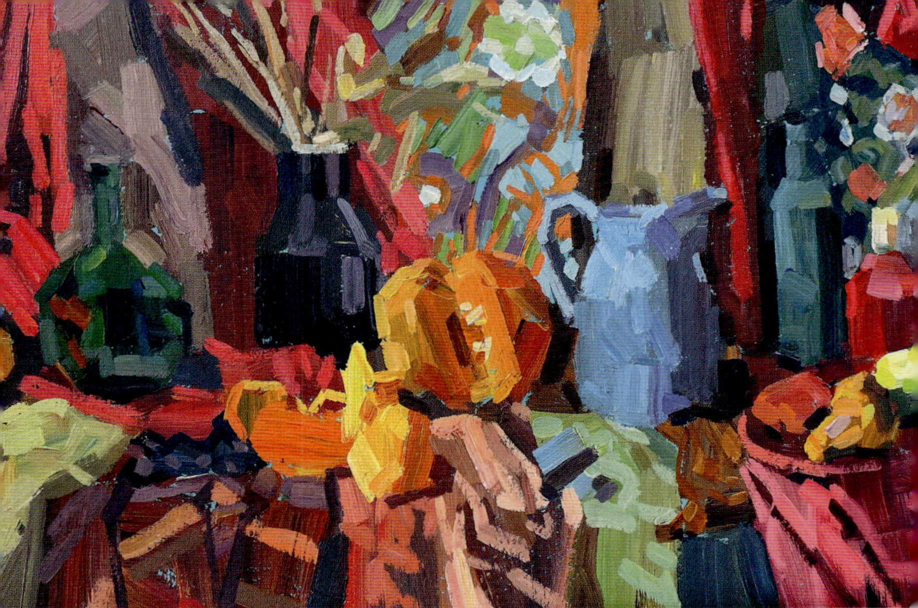

Using found images

Painting images you have found online can be a grey area for artists. The creator of the image will own the copyright, and if the subsequent image is painted unchanged and sold as-is – in essence, copied – then there may be an issue. However, if you come across something online that is perfect, then the following tips will help you to create your own artistic intepretation:

- Change the colours or, as shown in the examples here, combine parts of several images to make up a completely new one.

- Avoid photorealist copies by distorting shapes or stylizing elements. For example, lengthen or shorten a vase or jug, or add extra component parts or colours.

- Adapt the image with your own painting style, rather than doing a straight copy.

Copyright law

If you plan to sell or show your work in a public place, it is always safest to work from your own reference material. Art copyright law is complex and varies depending on where you are in the world. Check your local laws if you intend to use material you found online.

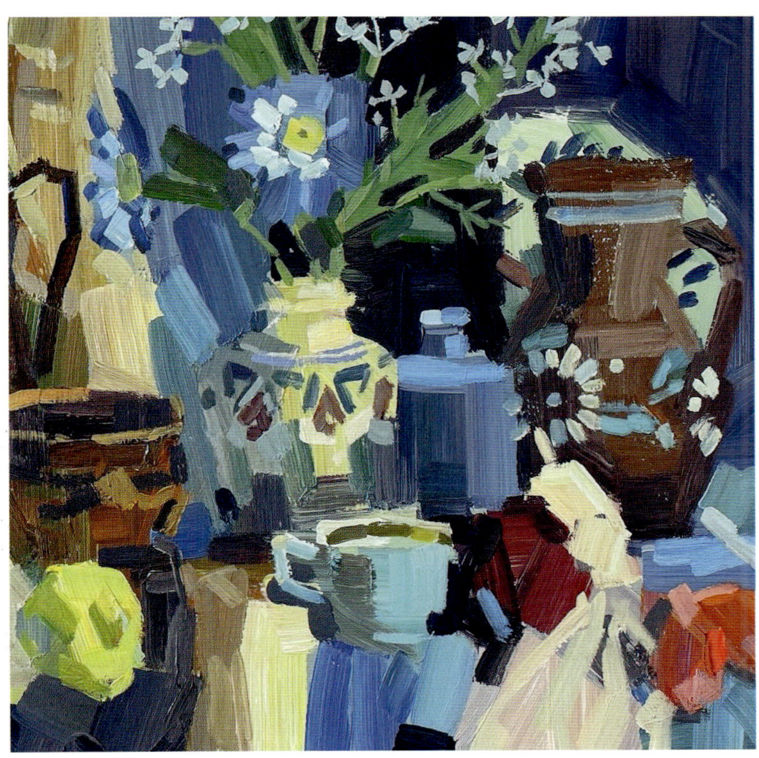

Opposite:

MAGENTA AND BLUE STILL LIFE

This page:

BLUE AND CREAM STILL LIFE

For these paintings I've combined elements and details drawn from a variety of images I found online. They have been carefully arranged and adapted to create a convincing sense of perspective and relative scale between the objects. This has allowed me to design the image, adding – for example – a lime green apple for a spot of colour or a choice of cloth for the patterns they contain.

Such collages of various elements are great for making up elaborate over-the-top still life paintings. You could go further by using all kinds of images retrofitted into one scene to create interesting landscapes or cityscapes.

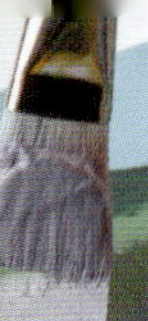

Unhappy accidents

Rare is the artist that has never applied a layer or made a brush mark that they haven't regretted. Trying to fix the problem by adding more paint can result in overworking and a sense of dissatisfaction.

If the issue isn't resolved quickly and the paint has dried, you'll have to live with the marks – unless the layer is thin enough, in which case you can simply paint over the error.

Beware – if you repaint areas multiple times you will fill in the texture and the paint will fail to adhere, sliding over the surface with very little grip. The colours will also look more dull.

QUICK FIX

If you spot a problem early enough and the paint is still very wet, you can strike quickly.

Wet a piece of kitchen paper or rag and gently dab off the paint, leaving a clean area. Allow to dry, then carry on with your painting.

RIP OFF THE STICKING PLASTER

I often repaint areas – even if the issues I spot are very large. Having learnt from the experience first time around, the reclaimed area is almost always markedly better.

It's easy to think of painting over an area as counterintuitive; as losing all your investment of effort and time. In reality, trying to tentatively resolve the issue with minimal change never quite works. Such an approach often develops into a frustrating and drawn-out process as you try to reclaim the flow other parts of the painting display.

It is better to be bold and decisive.

Take a break, make sure the area is completely dry, then come back with a plan.

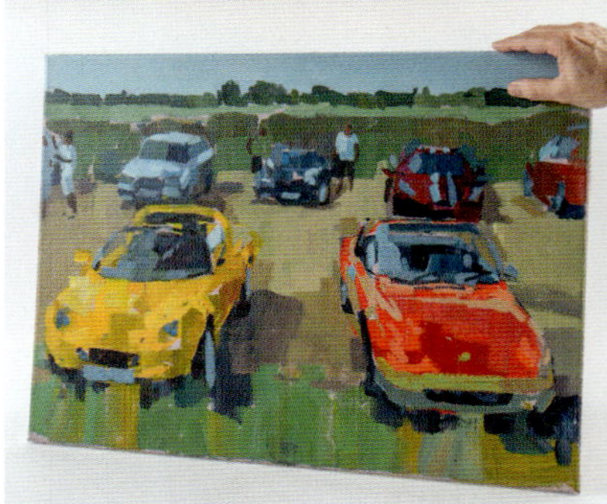

IDENTIFY THE PROBLEM, MAKE A PLAN

I wanted the car in the middle to be a lighter blue and the guy with the green t-shirt to have a purple t-shirt. I could just tweak these particular details, but experience has taught me to be decisive with changes.

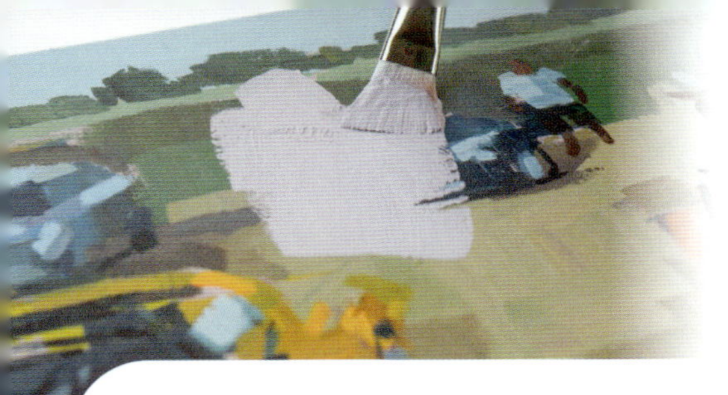

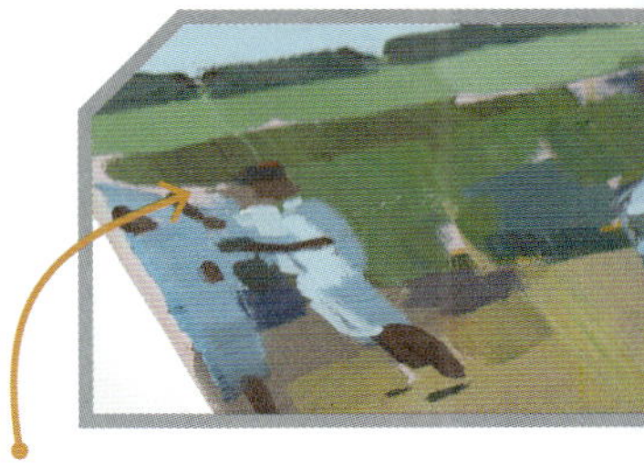

OVERPAINTING

When reworking problem areas, paint over it with the base colour (see page 68) or white. If the previous layer was thick, you might have some texture to contend with – although as long as you plan for it, this can prove helpful in the long run, creating interesting effects.

WHAT COLOUR?

You can see flashes of the base colour peeking through the painting here – but if your style creates more coverage, you'll probably be able to check the base colour from the sides of the painting.

IMPROVING THE PAINTING

Once the overpainting was dry, I sketched the car and figures again. I then applied the new colours, matching the foreground and background to the surroundings. Once the new additions were roughly painted in, I worked on refining the whole painting at the same time to meld the old with the new.

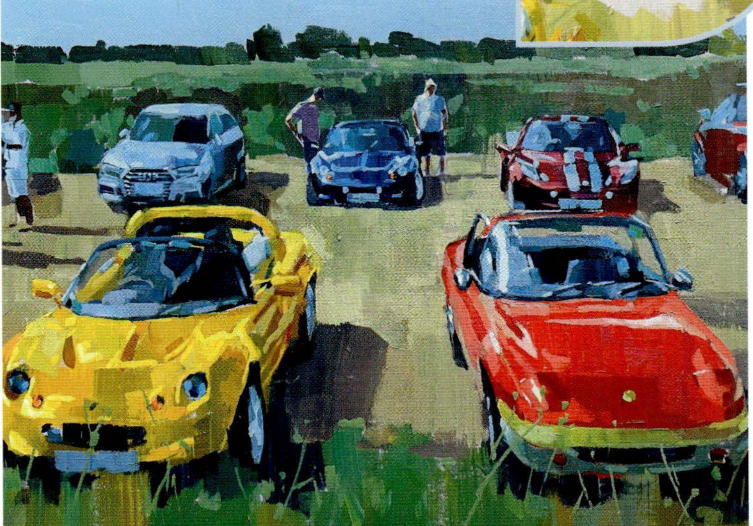

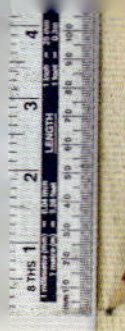

Finishing off

There's a huge advantage to painting on canvas if the artwork will later be shown in an exhibition: low expense. Unlike watercolour or pastel painting, you won't need glass (which generally makes up the largest expense in framing) to protect the painting. Acrylics don't require varnishing on completion, either – all they require is a good dusting now and then to stop dust building up on the artwork.

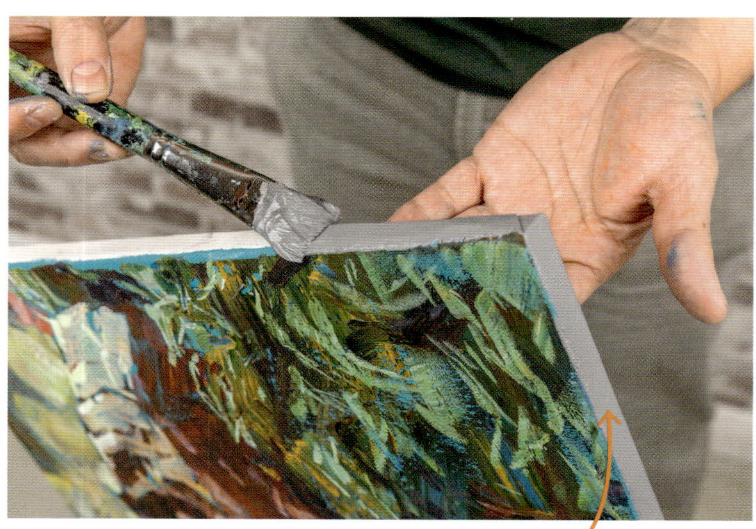

UNFRAMED WORK

You don't have to frame your work at all. I find a good alternative to framing is to paint the four edges of the canvas with Payne's gray. This links and creates a consistent look to your paintings.

NEUTRAL HUE

You don't need to use Payne's gray – you can use anything. However, bold colours tend to distract from the painting – or clash with the surface on which it's displayed – so it's usually best to use a neutral hue such as black, a pre-mixed grey or one you mix yourself.

FRAMED WORK

There are no hard and fast rules about framing, but in general frames should complement the artwork, not clash with or overwhelm them.

Framing can be extremely costly and take a while if you've employed a framer. I use an online mail order site which provides a choice of frames made to order, which are of surprisingly good quality. These come with all fixtures and fittings; you need only to screw the artwork into the frame. Most frames need some care and attention as they can become dented or chipped very easily. Wrap them in bubble wrap for safe keeping.

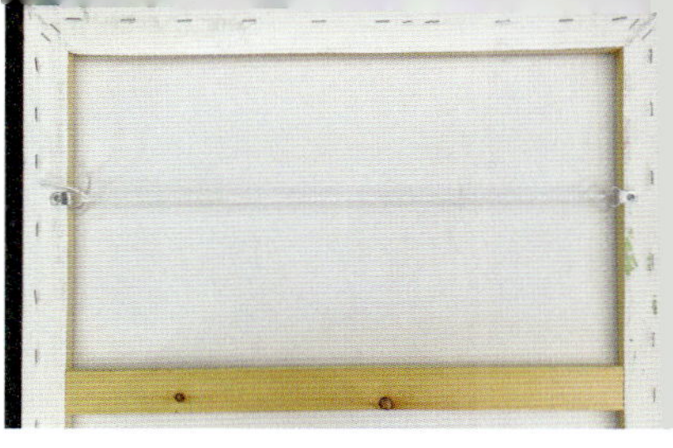

HANGING UNFRAMED WORK

Frames usually come with fixtures and fittings to help you hang your work. You can buy these separately for unframed work. In some cases you can simply run a cord behind, attaching it directly to the wooden support of the painting.

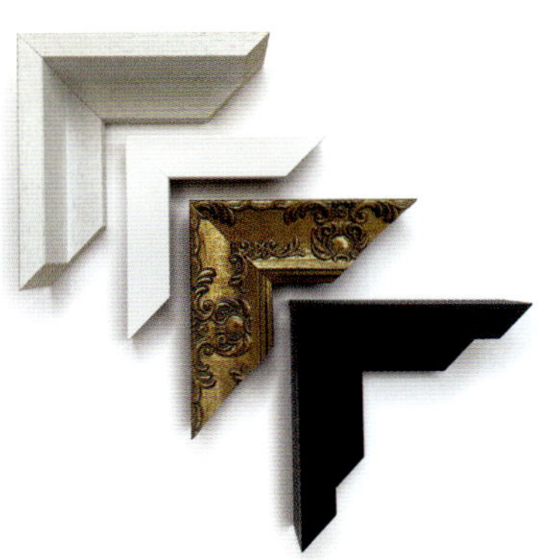

FRAMING OPTIONS

Pick a style and colour of frame that complements the painting as well as the walls or surrounding decoration it will hang beside.

My general rule is go for something simple, dark and chunky. Gold inlays or light frames can get shabby after a while. Lots of decoration can be too busy and plastic frames can look cheap.

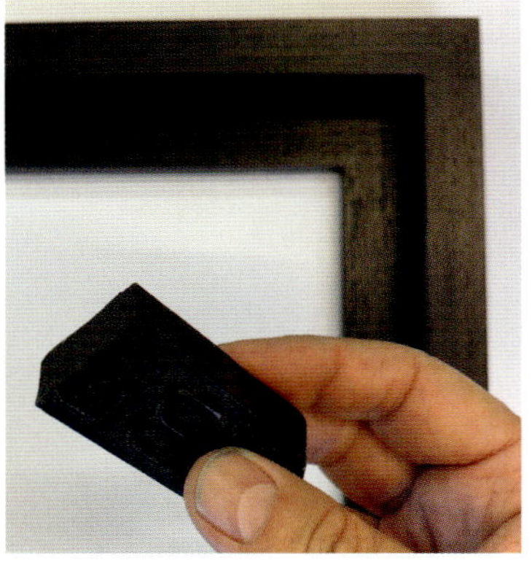

DARK FRAME ADVANTAGES

- *Dark wood frames mean tiny chips are easy to fix using a wax filler (shown above) or subtle applications of paint.*

- *Dark shoe polish can be used to polish them.*

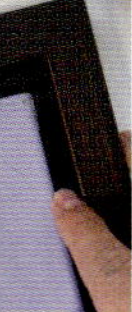

Floating frames

I always use a floating frame. In this sort of frame, a gap is left between the canvas and the edge of the frame, about a finger nail's width. This gives the appearance of floating.

You can fit the artwork in the frame yourself rather than going to a framer: buy a moulding/frame to fit the canvas, then use four screws to attach and two D-rings to hold the cord for hanging.

FITTING A FLOATING FRAME

1 On the back of the frame, make marks at the centre of each side and 5–10mm in from the inside edge. Use a screwdriver to drive in a screw at each mark until they just pierce the frame on the front side.

2 Align the artwork in the frame with a similar gap on each of the four sides. Once in place, tighten each screw to hold the artwork.

3 Next, screw the D-rings into the frame about a third of the way down the back of the canvas. Tie the cord between the D-rings and it's ready to hang.

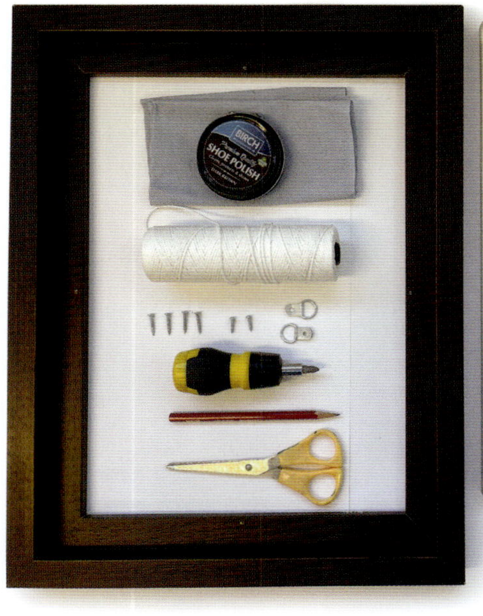

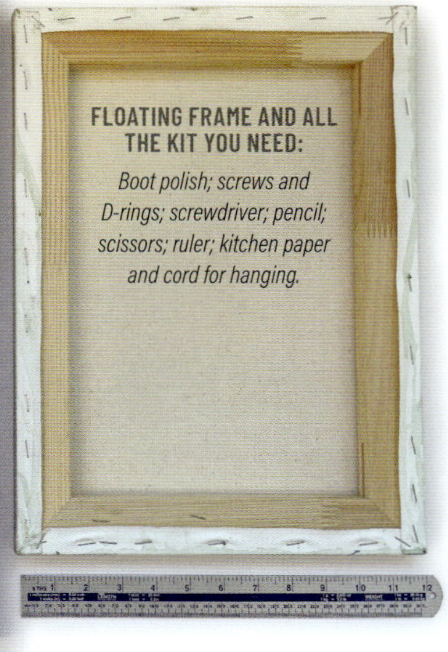

FLOATING FRAME

The canvas sits in the frame and screws are attached from behind the frame.

I order frames online with accessories and try to keep to consistent frame sizes. If the artwork doesn't sell first time around, I can recycle the frame for another time.

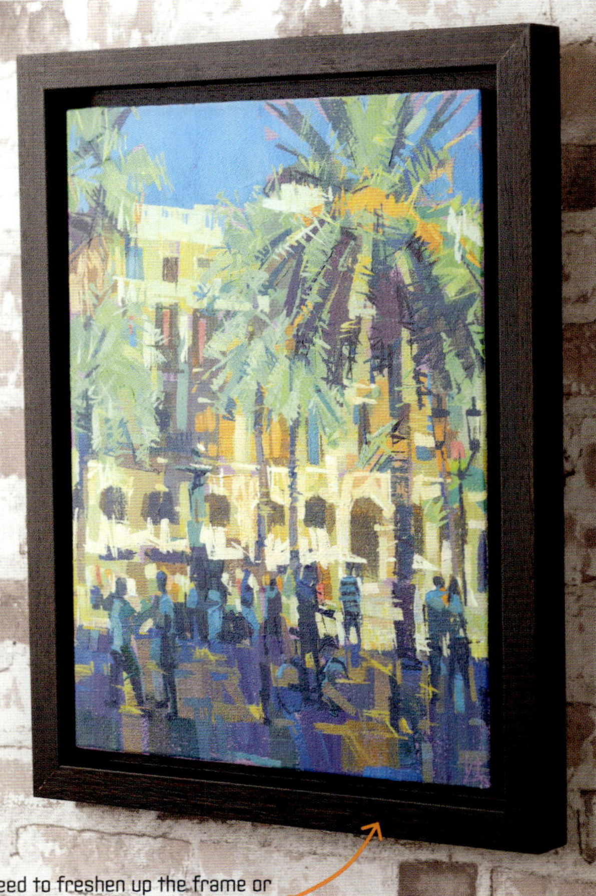

If you need to freshen up the frame or cover slight marks, just rub in a little boot polish.

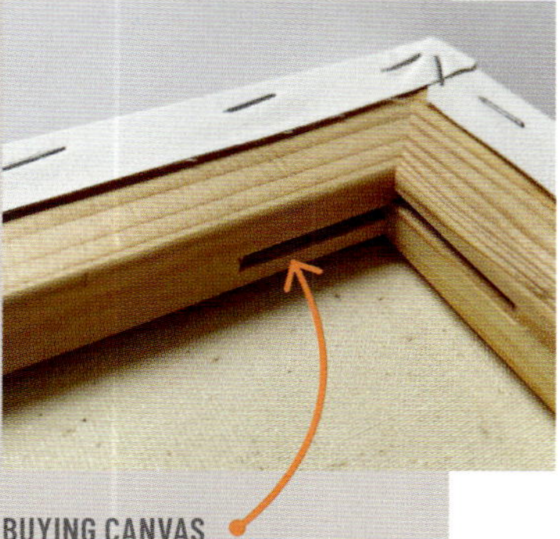

BUYING CANVAS

On the back of a box canvas, you'll usually see that the canvas is held in place on the frame with staples. In each corner you'll find a groove, and it's into these that you fit the wooden wedges.

SAGGY CANVAS

I've found linen canvases have a greater tendency to sag in the middle. This also happens where large amounts of paint on the canvas weigh it down. Larger canvases are more prone to sagging.

If there's a small sag when you first buy a canvas, try dripping a little water on the surface to solve the issue.

Canvas wedges

The most frequently asked question when I started running workshops, and the subject of the most viewed video on my art channel was:

'What are the pack of wooden wedges behind a canvas for?'

The answer is simple: the wedges are used to tighten the canvas if it begins to sag. You slot the wedges into the grooves to tighten the surface.

If you buy wooden stretchers and canvas to fit yourself, you'll need a nice snug fit. Use canvas pliers to hold the material in place along with a heavy-duty staple gun.

WHEN TO USE THE WEDGES

Happily, most of the time you won't need to use them. When you buy canvases, both student and artist qualities, you'll find that the canvas wrapped over the wooden stretchers provides a lovely taut surface to paint on. A good quality canvas should have a lovely drum sound when tapped on, showcasing a tight fit – you only need to use the wedges if it starts to sag.

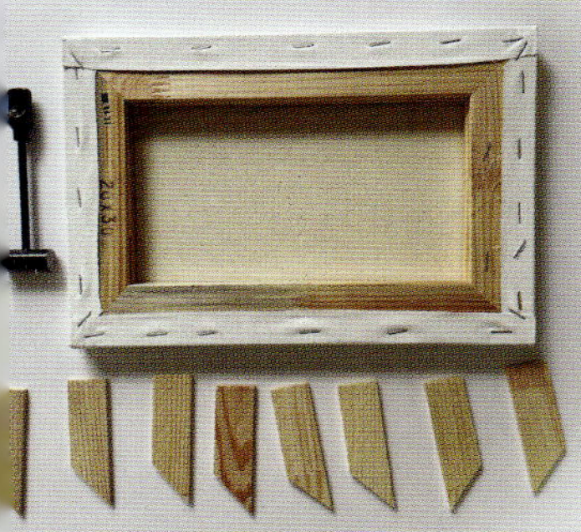

WHAT YOU NEED

Canvas, wedges and small hammer.

If you need to use the wedges, follow the steps below.

- The grooves can be very tight, so have a small hammer handy to gently tap the wedges in.

- In some instances, the wedges may be too small for the grooves and will fall out. Tap the wedges in as far as you can to hold them in place.

- Once all wedges are in the grooves you should find a nice taut canvas.

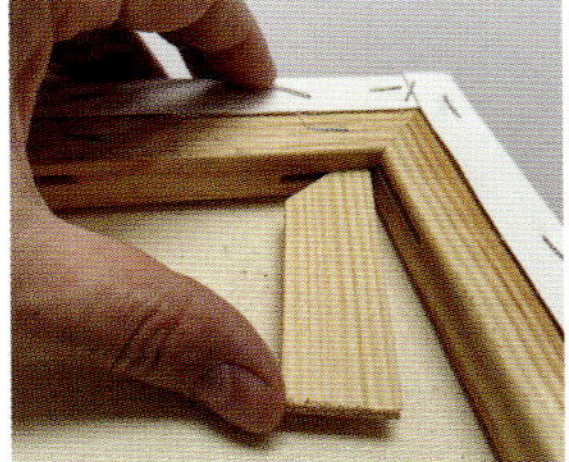

STAGE 1 Begin by slotting the wedge into the lower groove.

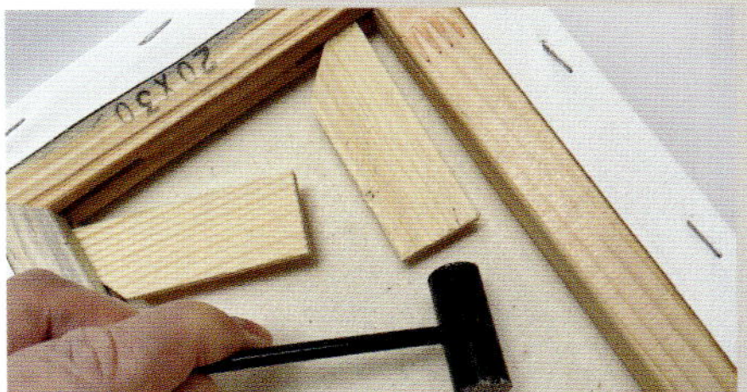

STAGE 2 Use a hammer if needed to drive the wedge in, then move on to the next. The wedges do not need to go all the way in, just enough to tighten the surface.

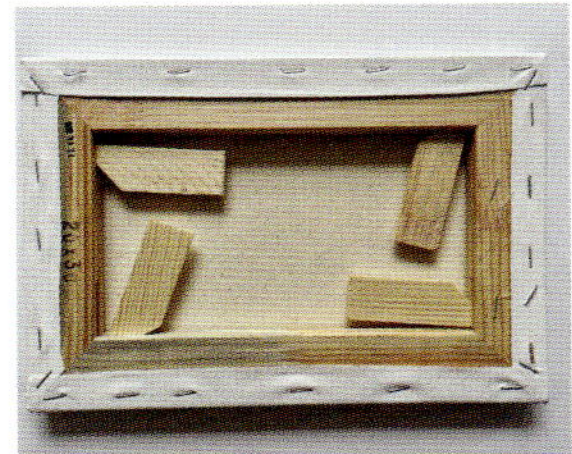

STAGE 3 Work round all the lower grooves in the same way, and check all the wedges are secure and firm.

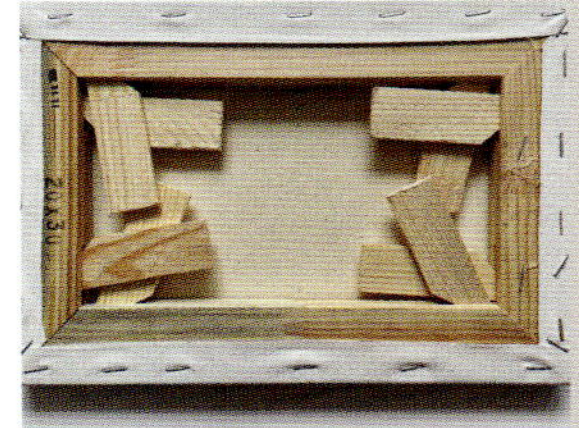

STAGE 4 Check the tightness, then repeat for the upper wedges. Check the canvas is taut. If not, tap them in a little more to finish.

Packaging artwork

Once you've created your artwork you might be lucky enough to sell it to a client, exhibit the work in a gallery or send it off as a gift. Whether framed or unframed, paintings – especially those under glass – require some consideration in packaging.

Some artists and galleries treat packaging extremely seriously – so even if you're delivering the work personally, try to avoid the artwork rattling around in the boot of your car. If you are sending it, remember that your courier won't be as invested as you are in the artwork, so make sure you package the artwork well.

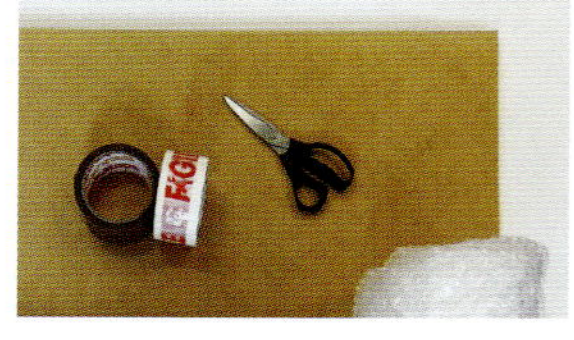

PACKING ESSENTIALS

For your average framed acrylic painting without glass, the essentials are as follows: bubblewrap, brown tape, 'Fragile' tape, a sheet or two of hardboard (ideally cut to size or close to size) and a cardboard box to package the work in.

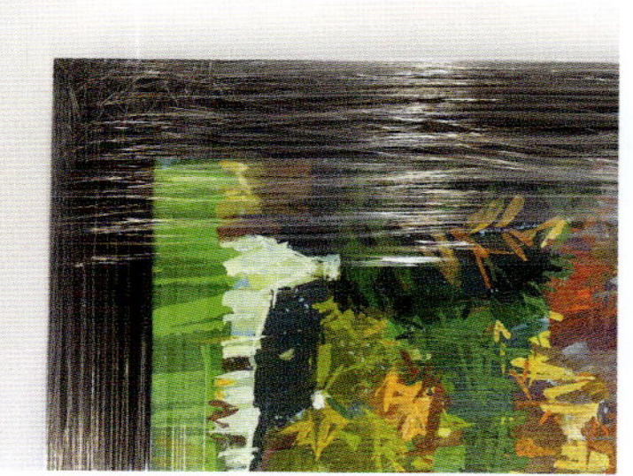

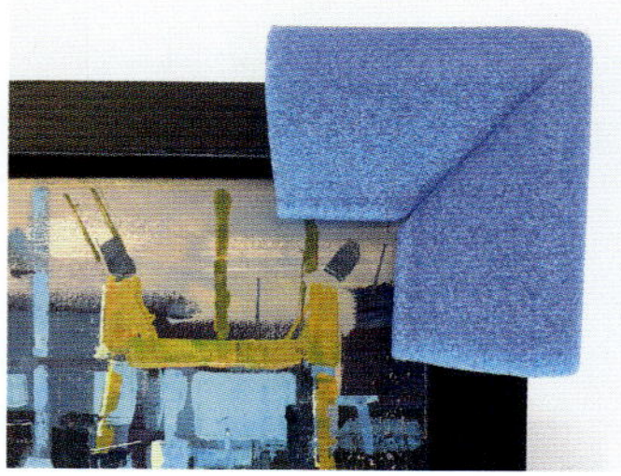

FRAME CORNER PROTECTION

The corners of picture frames are particularly susceptible to damage during transport. You can buy wrap-around tape for added frame protection (above left), as well as foam edges (above right) that slot around the frame to help protect it.

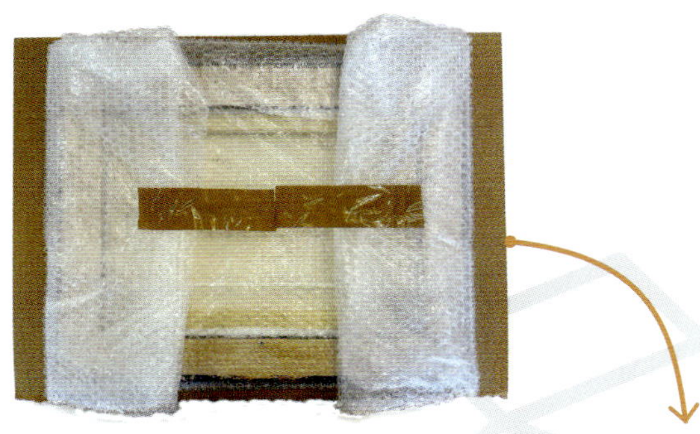

PROPERLY PACKAGED

Wrap it Start by wrapping the artwork in bubblewrap a couple of times, and tape securely.

Back it Tape a sheet or two of hardboard to the bubblewrapped artwork to secure it in place (see above).

Box it Place the artwork in the box – and if there's excess room, place scrap paper in the gaps to stop it from moving around.

Tape it Mark the box with 'Fragile' tape and you're ready to send or transport it.

Stiffy bags

'Stiffy' bags are reusable silver bubblewrap bags designed specifically for transporting artworks. They provide good protection and are quick and convenient.

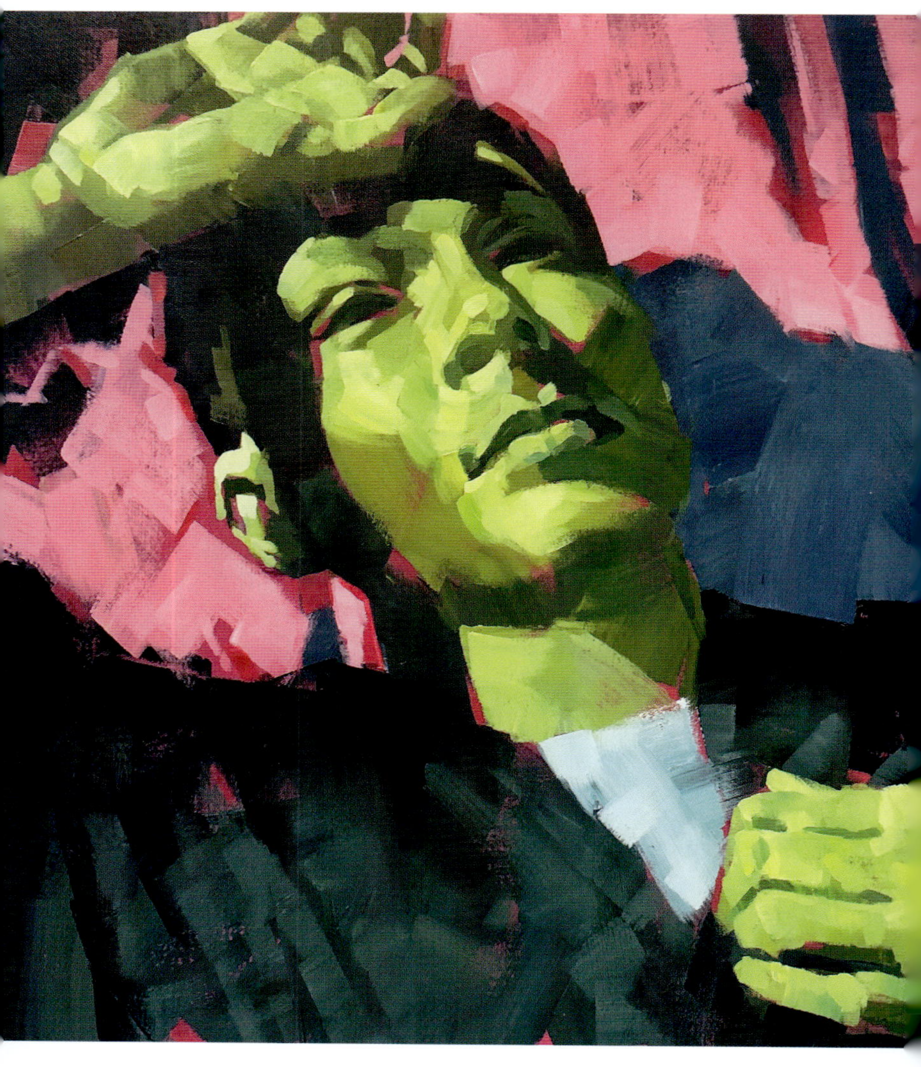

Being arty

Most amateur artists tend to begin with the foundations or mechanics of drawing and painting: the technicalities of drawing, painting, using tone and colour theory. However, what's considered 'arty' is more often categorized as an abstract concept, or a personal worldview showcased through one's work.

This can be confusing for those new to art, as the mechanics can almost be non-existent in favour of naïve or what some consider 'bad' drawing. The most important aspect is originality, either in technique or ideas. If you've seen dozens of realist animal paintings, a simplistic line drawing with distorted features will look original. You might still like the realistic ones – but the other stops you in your tracks and holds your attention.

Originality in conceptual choices tends to be seen as progressive or of higher value in certain galleries or institutions. It doesn't matter whether your reaction is good or bad – just that you're engaged.

Simple twists

As an example, this artwork is a relatively traditional portrait – the key difference is that it's in a non-representational colour scheme. It was an entry for a contemporary exhibition I had wanted to exhibit in for many years. Each year I entered an artwork based on completely traditional techniques; none made the exhibition. The conceptual twist of changing the colours in this entry was enough to make the artwork slightly more 'arty' or contemporary – and as a result it made it into the show.

The lesson is simple. When you're considering your artistic journey, bear in mind concepts as well as techniques – and work out how they'll play a part in your artworks.

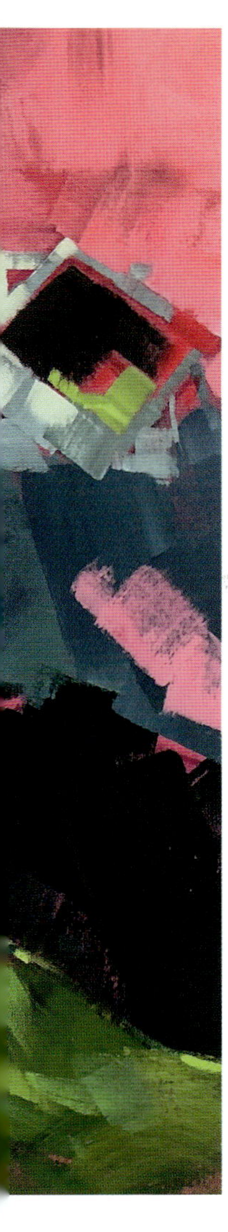

The most important aspect is originality, either in technique or ideas.

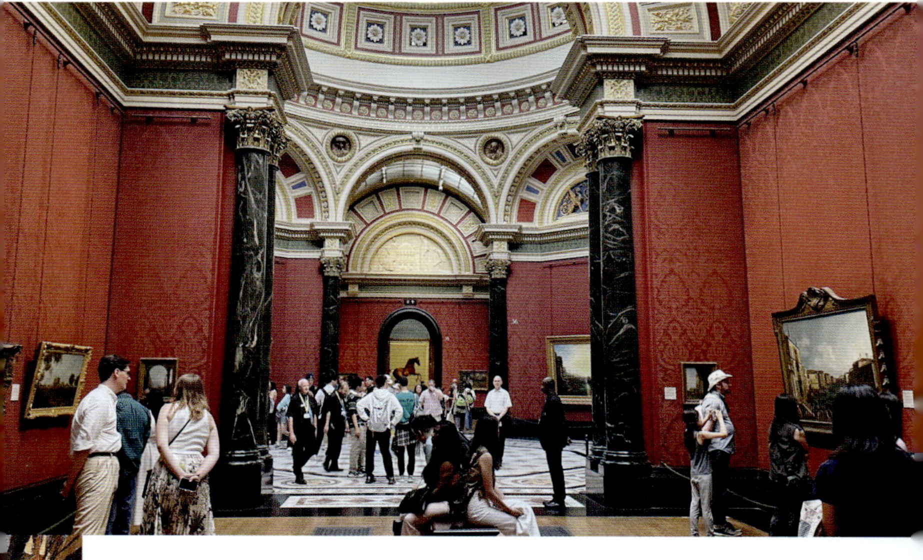

Staying inspired

I've drawn and painted since I was a child, continued into adulthood and it's been a career ever since. I find keeping inspired is easy: I love painting, so the fact that it pays the bills is a bonus. Painting is so much of my life that I think I'd struggle to do anything else.

Having taught painting for over fifteen years, I've found what inspires others to paint varies hugely, so if you don't know where to start, or are struggling for inspiration, here are some ways to reignite that desire to paint.

Art groups Joining an art group is a great way to be inspired as well as meeting others with similar interests. The joint sharing of ideas and constructive feedback – both positive and negative – is incredibly useful.

Demonstrations and courses Long or short art courses are great ways to gain personal insights into the process of artists you admire. Find some artists you like and see if they run courses or have social media channels. Be careful not to become a clone of those artists, and instead bounce off their ideas to fuel your own. Art groups sometimes have artist demonstrations where visiting artists showcase their technique for a couple of hours.

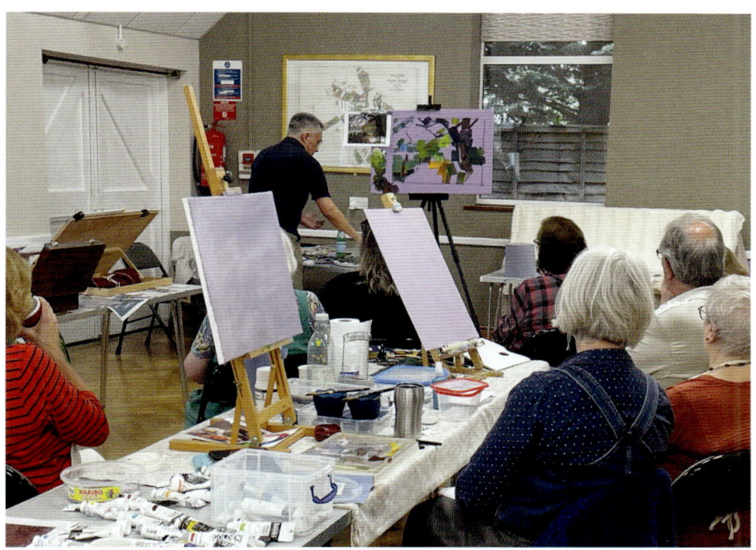

Galleries and online If you prefer painting on your own (my personal preference) then you'll spend ages online looking at artworks. This can be valuable, and I suggest that you also visit galleries in person. Some also run courses, both online and in-gallery. These are often art history-based and can offer great insights into eras of paintings or particular artists, their processes and techniques.

Isolation It's vital to turn off the noise occasionally and allow your own ideas to seep through. Set personal goals for your art to gauge improvements or failings.

Showcase Showing your work is daunting at first, but in order to evolve you need to experience how others relate to your work. You'll get criticism: some unwarranted, but some immensely positive.

Paint for pleasure First and foremost, paint for yourself. You will get your best results if you make your painting challenging, engaging and fun for yourself.

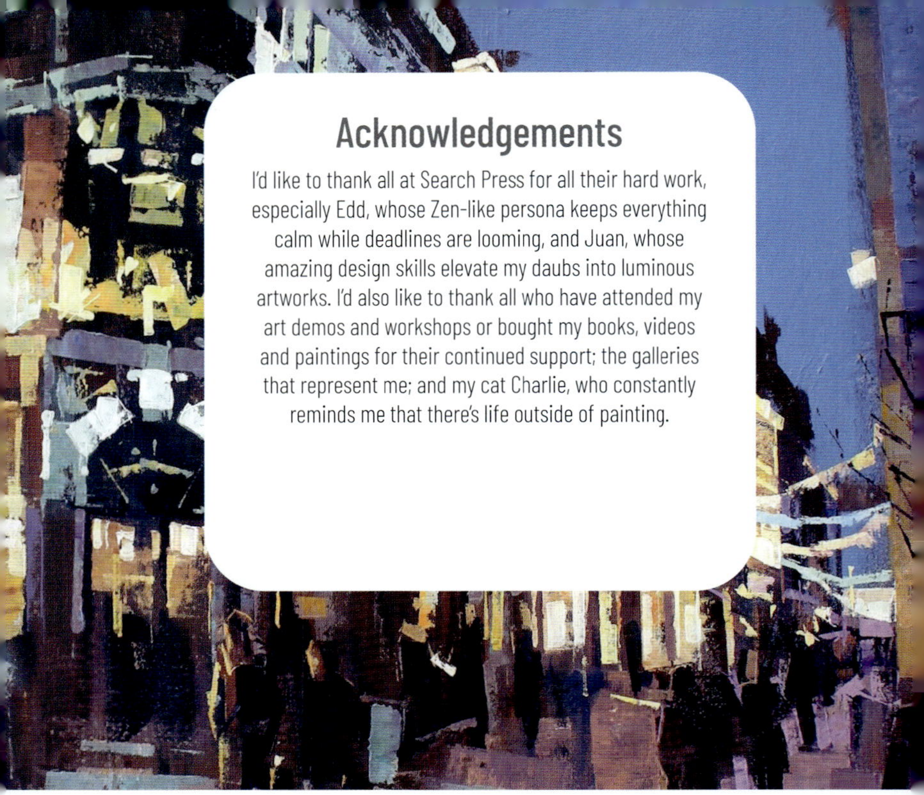

Acknowledgements

I'd like to thank all at Search Press for all their hard work, especially Edd, whose Zen-like persona keeps everything calm while deadlines are looming, and Juan, whose amazing design skills elevate my daubs into luminous artworks. I'd also like to thank all who have attended my art demos and workshops or bought my books, videos and paintings for their continued support; the galleries that represent me; and my cat Charlie, who constantly reminds me that there's life outside of painting.

First published in the UK 2025 by Search Press Limited, Wellwood, North Farm Road, Tunbridge Wells, Kent TN2 3DR

Text copyright © Hashim Akib 2025
Photographs by Mark Davison at Search Press Studios and author's own.
Photographs and design copyright © Search Press Ltd. 2025

ISBN: 978-1-80092-161-0
ebook ISBN: 978-1-80093-144-2

The Publishers and author can accept no responsibility for any consequences arising from the information, advice or instructions given in this publication.

Suppliers If you have any difficulty obtaining any of the materials and equipment mentioned in this book, visit the Search Press website for details of suppliers: www.searchpress.com

You are invited to the artist's website: www.hashimakib.co.uk

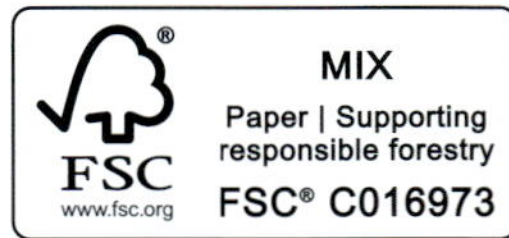

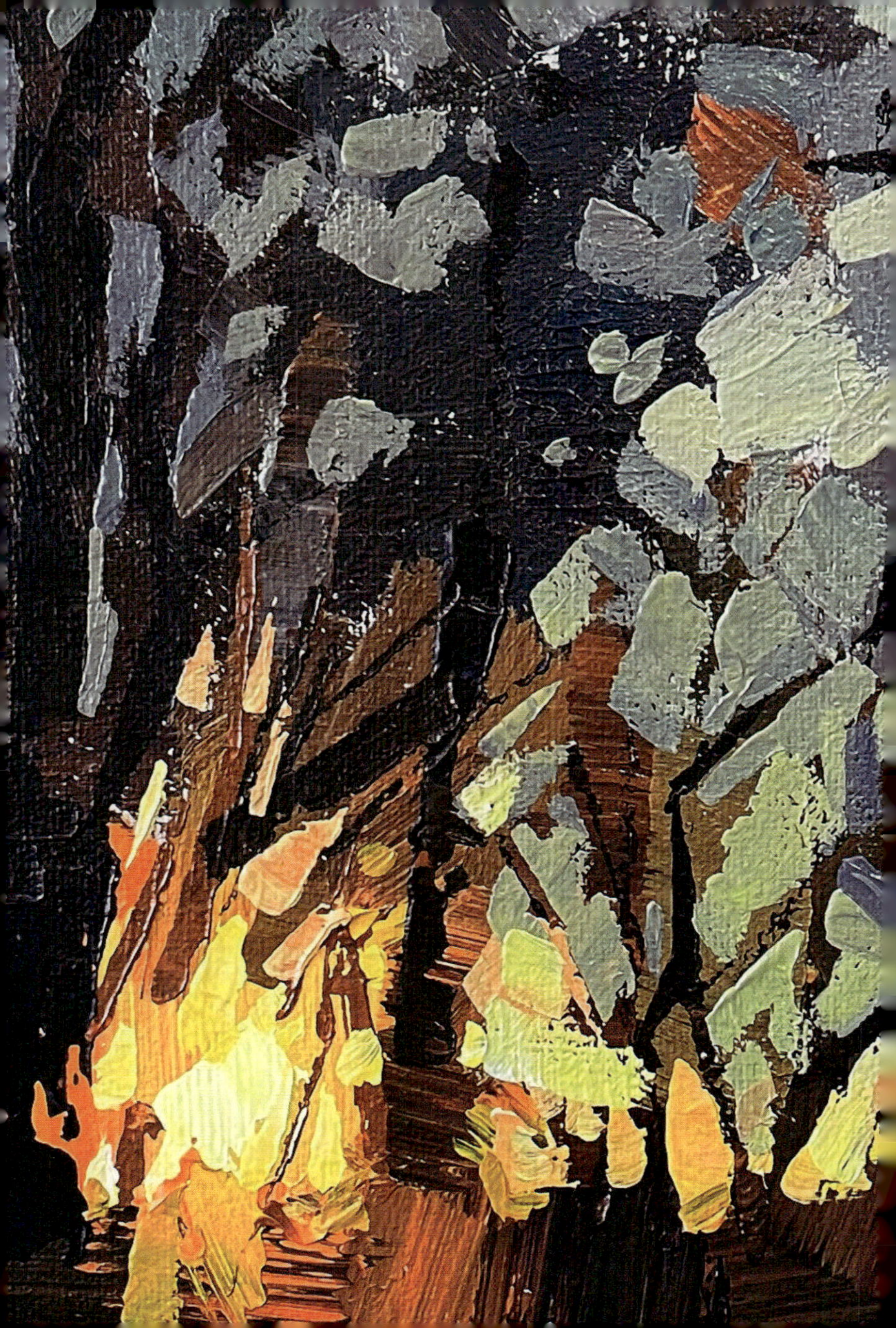